– The ESSENTIAL Source Book –

FORD
SMALL BLOCK
V8 RACING ENGINES
1962 to 1970

Des Hammill

OTHER GREAT BOOKS FROM VELOCE

Speedpro Series
4-Cylinder Engine Short Block High-Performance Manual – New Updated & Revised Edition (Hammill)
Alfa Romeo DOHC High-performance Manual (Kartalamakis)
Alfa Romeo V6 Engine High-performance Manual (Kartalamakis)
BMC 998cc A-series Engine, How to Power Tune (Hammill)
1275cc A-series High-performance Manual (Hammill)
Camshafts – How to Choose & Time Them For Maximum Power (Hammill)
Competition Car Datalogging Manual, The (Templeman)
Cylinder Heads, How to Build, Modify & Power Tune – Updated & Revised Edition (Burgess & Gollan)
Distributor-type Ignition Systems, How to Build & Power Tune – New 3rd Edition (Hammill)
Fast Road Car, How to Plan and Build – Revised & Updated Colour New Edition (Stapleton)
Ford SOHC 'Pinto' & Sierra Cosworth DOHC Engines, How to Power Tune – Updated & Enlarged Edition (Hammill)
Ford V8, How to Power Tune Small Block Engines (Hammill)
Holley Carburetors, How to Build & Power Tune – Revised & Updated Edition (Hammill)
Race & Trackday Driving Techniques (Hornsey)
Retro or classic car for high performance, How to modify your (Stapleton)
Secrets of Speed – Today's techniques for 4-stroke engine blueprinting & tuning (Swager)
Sportscar & Kitcar Suspension & Brakes, How to Build & Modify – Revised 3rd Edition (Hammill)
SU Carburettor High-performance Manual (Hammill)
V8 Engine, How to Build a Short Block For High Performance (Hammill)
Weber DCOE, & Dellorto DHLA Carburetors, How to Build & Power Tune – 3rd Edition (Hammill)

Essential Buyer's Guide Series
Cobra Replicas (Ayre)
Ford Capri (Paxton)
Ford Escort Mk1 & Mk2 (Williamson)
Ford Mustang – First Generation 1964 to 1973 (Cook)
Ford RS Cosworth Sierra & Escort (Williamson)

Those Were The Days ... Series
Motor Racing at Crystal Palace (Collins)
Motor Racing at Goodwood in the Sixties (Gardiner)
Motor Racing at Nassau in the 1950s & 1960s (O'Neil)
Motor Racing at Oulton Park in the 1960s (McFadyen)
Motor Racing at Oulton Park in the 1970s (McFadyen)
Motor Racing at Thruxton in the 1970s (Grant-Braham)

Rally Giants Series
Ford Escort MkI (Robson)
Ford Escort RS Cosworth & World Rally Car (Robson)
Ford Escort RS1800 (Robson)

Biographies
Amédée Gordini ... a true racing legend (Smith)
André Lefebvre, and the cars he created at Voisin and Citroën (Beck)
Cliff Allison, The Official Biography of – From the Fells to Ferrari (Gauld)
Edward Turner – The Man Behind the Motorcycles (Clew)
Jack Sears, The Official Biography of – Gentleman Jack (Gauld)
Jim Redman – 6 Times World Motorcycle Champion: The Autobiography (Redman)
John Chatham – 'Mr Big Healey' – The Official Biography (Burr)
The Lee Noble Story (Wilkins)
Pat Moss Carlsson Story, The – Harnessing Horsepower (Turner)
Tony Robinson – The biography of a race mechanic (Wagstaff)
Virgil Exner – Visioneer: The Official Biography of Virgil M Exner Designer Extraordinaire (Grist)

Toys & models
British Toy Boats 1920 onwards – A pictorial tribute (Gillham)
Diecast Toy Cars of the 1950s & 1960s (Ralston)
Ford In Miniature (Olson)
GM In Miniature (Olson)
Plastic Toy Cars of the 1950s & 1960s (Ralston)
Tinplate Toy Cars of the 1950s & 1960s (Ralston)

General
Alpine & Renault – The Development of the Revolutionary Turbo F1 Car 1968 to 1979 (Smith)
Alpine & Renault – The Sports Prototypes 1963 to 1969 (Smith)
Alpine & Renault – The Sports Prototypes 1973 to 1978 (Smith)
Autodrome (Collins & Ireland)
Autodrome 2 (Collins & Ireland)
Automotive Mascots (Kay & Springate)
Bluebird CN7 (Stevens)
BMC Competitions Department Secrets (Turner, Chambers & Browning)
British at Indianapolis, The (Wagstaff)
Chrysler 300 – America's Most Powerful Car 2nd Edition (Ackerson)
Chrysler PT Cruiser (Ackerson)
Cobra – The Real Thing! (Legate)
Concept Cars, How to illustrate and design (Dewey)
Cortina – Ford's Bestseller (Robson)
Coventry Climax Racing Engines (Hammill)
Daily Mirror 1970 World Cup Rally 40, The (Robson)
Dodge Challenger & Plymouth Barracuda (Grist)
Dodge Charger – Enduring Thunder (Ackerson)
Dodge Dynamite! (Grist)
Drive on the Wild Side, A – 20 Extreme Driving Adventures From Around the World (Weaver)
Dune Buggy, Building A – The Essential Manual (Shakespeare)
Dune Buggy Files (Hale)
Dune Buggy Handbook (Hale)
Fast Ladies – Female Racing Drivers 1888 to 1970 (Bouzanquet)
Fate of the Sleeping Beauties, The (op de Weegh/Hottendorff/op de Weegh)
Ferrari 288 GTO, The Book of the (Sackey)
Ford Cleveland 335-Series V8 engine 1970 to 1982 – The Essential Source Book (Hammill)
Ford F100/F150 Pick-up 1948-1996 (Ackerson)
Ford F150 Pick-up 1997-2005 (Ackerson)
Ford GT – Then, and Now (Streather)
Ford GT40 (Legate)
Ford Model Y (Roberts)
Ford Thunderbird From 1954, The Book of the (Long)
Formula 5000 Motor Racing, Back then ... and back now (Lawson)
Le Mans Panoramic (Ireland)
Lola – The Illustrated History (1957-1977) (Starkey)
Lola – All the Sports Racing & Single-seater Racing Cars 1978-1997 (Starkey)
Lola T70 – The Racing History & Individual Chassis Record – 4th Edition (Starkey)
Lotus 49 (Oliver)
Montlhéry, The Story of the Paris Autodrome (Boddy)
Motor Movies – The Posters! (Veysey)
Motor Racing – Reflections of a Lost Era (Carter)
Motor Racing – The Pursuit of Victory 1930-1962 (Carter)
Motor Racing – The Pursuit of Victory 1963-1972 (Wyatt/Sears)
Motorsport In colour, 1950s (Wainwright)
Northeast American Sports Car Races 1950-1959 (O'Neil)
Nothing Runs – Misadventures in the Classic, Collectable & Exotic Car Biz (Slutsky)
Pontiac Firebird (Cranswick)
Runways & Racers (O'Neil)
Sleeping Beauties USA – abandoned classic cars & trucks (Marek)
Speedway – Auto racing's ghost tracks (Collins & Ireland)
Standard Motor Company, The Book of the Supercar, How to Build your own (Thompson)
Tales from the Toolbox (Oliver)

Apps
Download now from
www.digital.veloce.co.uk

Hubble & Hattie
Animals and everything related to them!
www.hubbleandhattie.com

Books that explore any and every facet of military history
www.battlecry-books.com

eBooks
Download now from
www.digital.veloce.co.uk

www.veloce.co.uk

For post publication news, updates and amendments relating to this book please visit www.veloce.co.uk/book/V4425

First published in February 2014 by Veloce Publishing Limited, Veloce House, Parkway Farm Business Park, Middle Farm Way, Poundbury, Dorchester, Dorset, DT1 3AR, England.
Fax 01305 250479/e-mail info@veloce.co.uk/web www.veloce.co.uk or www.velocebooks.com

ISBN: 978-1-845844-25-7 UPC: 6-36847-04425-1

– The **ESSENTIAL** Source Book –

FORD SMALL BLOCK

V8 RACING ENGINES
1962 to 1970

(Veloce logo)

Des Hammill

Contents

Introduction & acknowledgements

INTRODUCTION

When the 221ci/3.6-litre small block V8 engine was being designed and developed in 1960, no thought whatsoever was given to its racing potential by the design group responsible. This was an all-new design of a stock engine with strict requirements to suit the all-new intermediate cars it was to power. The whole design criteria was based around minimum height and width dimensions, low weight, and, very importantly, low cost – this meant no surplus material of any description anywhere in the engine, which was achieved to a remarkable degree.

The 221ci engine was in production from July 1961 for fitting into 1962 model year Ford Fairlane and Mercury Meteor cars, and Carroll Shelby expressed an interest in the Fairlane V8 engine for installation into the AC Ace sports car late the same year. He was sent two 221ci engines for fitting trials, knowing that a larger

version would be available in a matter of weeks.

The 221ci engine was followed by the 260ci/4.2-litre version before the end of 1961, and Ford built a run of about 100 special versions of the 260ci known as the 'Hi-Performance 260.' Available in early 1962, it was these engines that powered the first 25 or so AC Cobra sports cars – and these units started to be used for applications other than stock passenger cars. Not many of these sports cars were sold in 1962, and the ones that raced were equipped with much modified Hi-Performance 260s.

Ford worked on a further small block derivative engine in 1962, the 289ci/4.7-litre. A Hi-Performance 289ci unit was also developed, to be produced in comparatively large numbers, both as a replacement for the Hi-Performance 260, and as an option in production cars to spread the cost of production.

The Hi-Performance 289 engine was available to Carrol Shelby early

in 1963, and also in 1963 model year Ford Fairlanes from March the same year. Shelby American used the Hi-Performance 289 engine to power its two Daytona Coupes at the 1964 Le Mans with remarkable success.

From mid-1962, Ford also began the development of an all-aluminium, 255ci/4.2-litre version of the cast iron 260ci V8 engine, specifically designed for the prestigious 1963 Indianapolis 500 race that Ford and Lotus were teaming up to try and win. The 255ci engine was very successful at the event, and powered a Lotus 23 driven by Jim Clark into second place.

In 1964 a 255ci pushrod Indianapolis engine powered the Ford GT at the Nürburgring 1000km, but was replaced by modified Hi-Performance 289s for the Le Mans event. Despite not winning, the engines certainly gave an extremely good account of themselves; all three cars ultimately broke down with failures unrelated to the engines themselves.

In 1963/1964 Ford developed the 255ci pushrod Indianapolis V8 into a four valve per cylinder, double overhead camshaft engine that powered a Lotus to victory in the 1965 Indianapolis 500.

By 1965 Ford had, to a degree, sidelined the small block engine for use at Le Mans, and instead concentrated on the 427ci/7.0-litre FE big block engine it had already spent a lot of money developing for racing. The big block units ultimately prevailed and were used to power the MkII GT-40s – the Ford GT had a name change for 1965 when it then became known as the Ford GT-40.

With the introduction of the 1965 Mustang in the middle of the 1964 model year, Shelby American began racing Hi-Performance 289 engine versions with much success.

In 1966 Ford introduced special FE coded racing parts for the Hi-Performance 289, such as stronger than stock block and main caps to increase reliability, and larger port and valve cylinder heads to increase power output. More specialised racing parts were introduced in 1967, such as a forged steel crankshaft, four-bolt main cap block, and Cooper mechanical joint 'O'-ring and periphery mattress head gasket system.

For the 1968 Le Mans the GT-40 was required to use an engine of no more than 302ci/5.0-litres. Ford adhered by installing a small block engine of this size, and used the same car to win the great race that year and the next.

Due to the success of the 427ci 'Tunnel Port' engine in NASCAR, Ford Division requested the Engine and Foundry Division transfer the technology to the small block engine for Trans-Am racing. This was done

against the advice of the Engine Engineering engineers and, although there were many evolutionary innovative features incorporated into these engines, such as the dry-deck Cooper mechanical joint 'O'-ring head gasket system, the same as the 1963 Indianapolis 500 255ci pushrod engine, the 'Tunnel Port' 302ci was not a success in circuit racing.

Ford Division asked the Engine and Foundry Division to produce a suitable engine for 1969 after the failure of the Tunnel Port 302ci engine in sedan racing in 1968. The subsequent Boss 302ci was a combination of the existing 302ci small block fitted with the cylinder heads from the Cleveland V8 engine still under development. This resulted in a competitive engine for 1969, and a Ford Mustang driven by Parnelli Jones winning the 1970 Trans-Am Series.

In November 1970 Ford management decided to withdraw from motor racing and, with the exception of a few assistance packages, Ford was out of racing for the next decade.

ACKNOWLEDGEMENTS
It would not have been possible to share the true reasoning and technical information behind the development of these engines without the invaluable help received from the many now retired Ford Engine Engineering career engineers involved in the work and decision making at the time, who agreed to be interviewed for this book.

In far too many instances in the past, assumptions have been made or conjecture used, which has resulted in incorrect or misleading information entering the public domain.

Further acknowledgements
Ford literature *Road Racing the Ford 289 High Performance Engine (1967), 1965 Ford Double Overhead Cam Competition Engine* and *Boss 302 Engine Modifications for Strip And Track (1970)* are reproduced courtesy of the Ford Motor Company; Chris Sawyer; Alex Mishura, Ford Australia; Ronald Sears, Powertrain Staff Technical Specialist for crankshaft systems, Ford USA; Paul Kynaston of Kynaston Auto-Services Exeter, England; Ian Richardson of Wildcat Engineering, Rhydiaman, North Wales; Ford engineer Mose Nowland of Ford Racing; John Keene of Ford New Zealand; Ray Herron, Tom Magyur, John Cloor and Marty Kot of Ford Racing Technical USA. The following ex-Ford Engine Engineering engineers; Hank Lenox, Bill Barr, Joe Macura, George Stirrat, Wally Beaber, Bob Corn, Ralph Rays, Elio Lori, Ray Doute, Bud Hebets, Roman Kuzma, Lee Morse, Lee Dykstra, Mitch Marchi and Robert Mrdjenovich; Rick Williams of Ford USA; Bob Mead of Balancing Specialties, New Lynn, New Zealand; George Sheweiry of New Zealand; Ivan Segedin of New Zealand; Mark Reynolds of the Ford Galaxie Club of America; Robert McLellan of *McLellan's Automotive History*; Bob Mannel, author of *Mustang and Ford Small Block V8, 1962-1969* (www.smallblockford.com), who was most helpful, and spent a great deal of time to give me a much better understanding of the 1960s small block Ford V8 parts situation (his book contains all relevant part, engineering and casting alphanumeric codes, and casting date codes of the listed years [e-mail bobmannel@charter.net. Tel: 423-245-6678 [USA]]; Lynn Park, Steve Beck, John Morton, Ryan Falconer, Pete Brock, Andy Neilson, Drew Neilson, Dan Gurney and Phil Remington of All American Racers; Ex-Shelby American engine builders Jim O'Leary and Jack Hoare; Joe Mondello of Mondello Porting Services; Lee Holman, Jim Rose

and Larry Wallace of Holman & Moody, Charlotte, North Carolina, USA; KB-Silv-O-Lite technical, United Engine and Machine Co, Carson City, NV 89706, USA (e-mail tech@kb-silvolite.com.

Tel: 1-800-648-7970/1-775-882-7790); Sig Erson, Bud Moore, Parnelli Jones, Mike Daniels, Noel Manton and Donald Silawsky. My most grateful thanks to Sally Stocker for proofreading and

rewriting the text of this book. Thanks to the SAE for permission to reprint *SAE 818A - A Ford Engine For Indianapolis Competition* and *SAE S397 - The Ford D.O.H.C. Competition Engine*.

Chapter 1
Hi-Performance 260s of 1962

The 221ci small block engine had been in production for four months when Carroll Shelby expressed an interest in a high-powered version for his AC sports car project in 1961, and Ford began a performance development of the soon to be released larger capacity 260ci version to specifically comply with his requirements. The same group of engineers that had developed the stock 221ci and 260ci two-barrel carburettor engines worked on the high-performance 260ci four-barrel carburettor units, which were delivered to Shelby in number from February 1962.

Carroll Shelby again approached Ford management, seeking a high-performance version of the 260ci engine. Ford readily accepted, realising the opportunity to compete with the Chevrolet Corvette and enhance its own image. This was the beginning of Ford's association with Carroll Shelby, and the resulting Hi-Performance 289ci engine was used to win the 1965 World Sports Car Championship, among many other top class championship successes.

The 'Hi-Performance 260' – a little-known version of the Ford 260ci small block V8 engine – was rated by Ford at 260bhp at 5800rpm with 269lb-ft of torque at 4800rpm, or one horse power per cubic inch of displacement. A special order of approximately 100 of these high-performance 260ci engines was produced at the Cleveland Engine Plant. The engines featured a four-barrelled Holley or 4100 Autolite carburettor with an automatic choke, a cast iron inlet manifold, 9.2:1 compression ratio, a mechanical camshaft with 0.477in of valve lift, single valve springs with a flat wound damper, 85lb seated pressure and 235lb of open pressure, the stock one-piece sintered valve spring retainers, a dual-point distributor with inoperative vacuum advance even though the canister was in place, and stock 260ci cast iron exhaust manifolds.

Stock cylinder heads planed by 0.024in were used to increase the compression ratio. The short assemblies of these engines were the same as any stock 260ci engine, with no special parts added or substituted – as many stock components as possible were used to minimise cost.

With the exception of the exhaust manifolds, these engines were installed in the first AC Cobra road-going cars as they came from Ford. Carroll Shelby replaced the standard Ford exhaust manifolds with four individual cast iron 'Y' alternatives which AC Cars in England had manufactured specifically for this application. The new manifolds were fitted two per side of the engine, with steel tubing pipes coming off them that turned rearward under the car, bifurcated into one main pipe, although some of the engines were equipped with custom-made tubular steel exhaust manifolds, such as those made by Belanger or Hooker, instead.

Hi-Performance 260 engines were also fitted to Rally versions of the Ford Falcon Sprint and Mercury Comet cars, but only up to 20 units (not 75, as is often reported) because 1962 was a poor year for AC Cobra sales. Few original examples of these cars exist now. The Hi-Performance 260 engines were not in use after the Hi-Performance 289 was introduced, so the units in many of these cars were replaced with the larger and more powerful 289ci version of the small block engine. This very limited production Hi-Performance 260 engine was without a doubt the forerunner of the production Hi-Performance 289 engines of 1963-1967, despite only the mechanical camshaft and lifters, dual-point distributor, inlet manifold and carburettor criteria actually being carried over.

Chapter 2
Hi-Performance 289s of 1963-1967

The production Hi-Performance 289 was fitted into 1963 and 1964 model year Ford Fairlanes listed in sales literature as a '271-hp Challenger 4-V/289 High Performance V-8,' and in 1965 model year Fairlanes as a '271-hp High Performance Challenger V-8.' The engine was fitted into as many as 1000 June-July 1964 mid-year introduction 1965 model year Ford Mustangs as a '271-hp 4V/289 High Performance V-8,' and was available as an option through 1966 and 1967 model year Ford Mustangs up until the end of July of that year as a '271-hp Challenger Hi-Performance V-8' or '271-hp Cobra V-8.' It was available as a special order in all 1964 and 1965 model year Mercury Comet cars except station wagons, and was fitted into about seven or eight 1965 model year Falcons destined for Canada.

There were several factors which set these engine blocks apart from the stock 289ci two-barrel or slightly

later introduced four-barrel carburettor versions of the same basic engines. A Hi-Performance 289 engine block was a stock production C3AE-6015-N for 1963 model year cars, C4OE-6015-C and C4OE-6015-F for 1964 model year cars, and C5AE-6015-E for 1965-1967 model year cars. The units had a two-bolt block with larger two-bolt main caps fitted. The main caps were also made out of stronger, 80% nodular iron material, as opposed to the plain grey cast iron of the stock two-bolt items. The front oil gallery plugs were press-in and the rear ones were screw-in, as per all stock 289ci blocks (not all screw-in as has often been stated). The crankshafts on the Hi-Performance 289 were identical to those on the stock 221ci, 260ci and 289ci, having been made using the very same moulds, although these were made from Ford's 80% nodular iron as opposed to the listed stock 30/40% nodular iron.

These crankshafts were all checked for their amount of nodularity by polishing an area of the rearmost counterweight – namely the outer edge – and an inspector viewing the surface through a magnifier. The inspectors carried a series of photographs demonstrating what the various percentages of nodularity should look like, so would compare the view through the magnifier to the photograph of 80% nodular iron. This visual comparison was the quickest and cheapest way to ascertain the approximate nodularity of these components. If a crankshaft didn't come up to the required nodularity, it was rejected and put into a melt for stock production crankshafts. A genuine Hi-Performance 289 crankshaft is therefore technically very easy to identify because of the polished rear counterweight, plus a daubing of orange paint.

Orange was the colour paint used

in the plant to identify Hi-Performance 289 engine parts at a glance. This was an engine manufacturing plant initiative and nothing to do with a design/drawing requirement. The orange paint was placed on the third counterweight in from the rear of the crankshaft.

These Hi-Performance 289 crankshafts were balanced with the same bob-weights on each big end journal as used to balance the regular 221ci, 260ci and 289ci versions, and are therefore identical as manufactured. The front and rearmost counterweights of all crankshafts were slightly heavier than they needed to be as manufactured, so there was always an amount of material to be removed during the balancing process.

The Hi-Performance 289 was fitted with stronger connecting rods that were heavier than stock versions. The difference in weight was made up for in the amount of external balance these engines had fitted to the flywheel/flexplate. The supplementary counterweight and crankshaft damper was 30.4oz-in versus the 28.2oz-in of the stock two- and four-barrel 289ci.

Although the connecting rods were stronger, the actual connecting rod forging was the stock CAE3-D 289ci item, with upgraded connecting rod cap and bolts. The big end bearing shells of all Hi-Performance 289 engines were better quality than the stock engine components, and coded C3OE-6211-AB. The connecting rod was machined to take a ⅜in diameter bolt in conjunction with a new stronger twin rib C2OE-B coded connecting rod cap, which was slightly larger in places to suit the ⅜in bolt and nut. Less material was machined off the width of the connecting rod, so those on the Hi-Performance 289 were wider than stock by between 0.080-0.100in, and they remained broached like stock late 260ci

and 289ci items where the head of the connecting rod bolt rests.

The 221ci, 260ci and 289ci engines all used connecting rods with the same centre-to-centre distance of 5.155in, and, as they used a 2.870in stroke crankshaft, had a 1.78:1 connecting rod to stroke ratio.

The early Hi-Performance 289 engine connecting rod bolts had a radius edge and a flat edge. Later items were the same rectangular shape as stock versions, only a bit larger and with chamfered top edges. The radius edge of the early connecting rod bolt head was positioned in the connecting rod adjacent to the 'I' beam, which at first glance looks to be the wrong way round, perhaps. It isn't – if the bolts were fitted this way round, the nuts tended to come loose. The first bolts used on Hi-Performance 289 connecting rods were, in fact, out of a 352ci FE Ford V8 engine. Ford introduced the second type of connecting rod bolts in January of 1964, specific to this engine to avoid any confusion over which way the head of the bolt was to be fitted. The connecting rod nut remained the same. The early bolts were used exclusively 1963 to January 1964. A 1964 model year Hi-Performance 289 engine produced after January 1964 could have either bolt type fitted as a set. Engines from about January 1965 were equipped with the later bolts.

The Hi-Performance 289 connecting rods weighed on average 595g without bearing shells, which is about 30g more than the late 260ci and early 289ci stock items. With bearing shells they weighed about 632g. The different cap, connecting rod bolts and nuts, as well as less material being machined off the width of the connecting rod, contributed to increased big end weight. Ford engineers added material

to the connecting rods where necessary to improve durability and minimise weight gain.

Ford fitted Autothermic-type pistons to its Hi-Performance 289 engines. These items differed from stock 289ci pistons in that they were flat-topped, with four valve reliefs for fitting into either cylinder bank, and made by Bohn Aluminium & Brass from a stronger aluminium material than stock.

The stock Autothermic steel strut pistons used in 289ci engines tended to develop cracks in the piston skirts around the 75,000-100,000 mile mark. After 125,000m you could expect to see cracks on one, two or three pistons emanating from the same point on the lower edge of the skirt. As a general rule, the higher the rpm the engine had been turning at the lower the mileage when cracks would start to develop, always on the same side of the piston.

Although produced from the same material and to the same physical size as stock 289ci engine items, Hi-Performance 289 flywheels were balanced to a different amount of external balance (30.4 oz-in), so were specific to the engine. These flywheels were tested to be 'burst-proof' at 12,000rpm for two minutes, and had orange paint daubed on them in the factory for identification purposes.

The crankshaft damper was also unique to the Hi-Performance 289 engine. It was much wider and had a higher inertia rating than stock items, with a 6½in maximum diameter, stepped down once, and 1¹¹⁄₁₆in width, specifically 'tuned' to 'respond' to the torsional vibration factor of the engine. Hi-Performance 289 engines were also fitted with a supplementary counterweight plate at the front of the crankshaft, between the crankshaft's front main bearing journal and the narrow ½in timing chain sprocket that went with it. The damper and supplementary counterweight were used together to maintain the required external balance amount at the front of the engine – one can't be used without the other. The crankshaft damper, supplementary counterweight and narrow camshaft sprocket were all specific to the Hi-Performance 289 engine, so would not interchange by straight substitution onto a stock 289ci two-barrel or 289ci four-barrel carburettor engine – it would not have the correct balance.

The cylinder heads on the Hi-Performance 289 engine differed from stock two-barrel carburettor 289ci versions by having a different combustion chamber shape that produced an approximate 10.5:1 compression ratio. Two versions existed between March 1963 and June 1964. Cylinder heads fitted to engines produced between March 1963 and April 1964 had a C3OE-E or C3OE-F casting code, with an inlet valve head diameter of 1.670in, exhaust valve head diameter of 1.450in, and combustion chamber volume of 49.2cc. Cylinder heads fitted to engines produced between April and June 1964 had a casting code of C4OE-B and were made to a different specification. The exhaust valve head diameter remained the same, but the inlet valve head diameter was increased to 1.780in. The combustion chamber was modified to accommodate the larger inlet valve heads by having a slightly different shape and its volume increased to 54.5cc. Compression ratio was reduced from 10.5:1 to 10.0:1.

All 289ci engines (including the Hi-Performance) used the same valves from the beginning of April 1964. With the introduction of 1965 model year cars the casting code changed to C5OE-A. No changes were made for the 1966 model year. Cylinder heads fitted to 1967 model year engines had a new casting code of C7ZE-A, as the exhaust passageways had been altered to allow thermactor machining for cars destined for California. The later C8ZE-B cylinder heads were service replacements, and the exhaust passageways were all machined for thermactor.

The Hi-Performance 289 cylinder heads all featured raised, cast-in valve spring seats to positively locate the base of the outside diameter of the outer valve springs, and screw-in rocker studs as opposed to press-in ones. The seated valve spring pressure was 83-92lb at an installed height of 1.770in, and the 'over the nose' or fully open pressure was 235-259lb at a compressed valve spring height of 1.320in. The valve springs were strong singles with a flat wound damper fitted inside them, and stronger than stock flat-top, one-piece steel valve spring retainers unique to the Hi-Performance 289 engine.

The camshaft was mechanical, with 275 degrees of duration and 0.477in of valve lift. It was phased so that the inlet valves opened 25 degrees before top dead centre (BTDC) and closed 70 degrees after bottom dead centre (ABDC). The exhaust valves opened 73 degrees before bottom dead centre (BBDC) and closed 22 degrees after top dead centre (ATDC). This Hi-Performance 289 camshaft proved to be unique with its low degrees of overlap (when the exhaust and inlet valves are open together), which enabled the engines to have very good pick up from comparative low rpm, and an approximate 4000rpm power band.

A supplementary counterweight was fitted at the front of the Hi-Performance 289 engine between the front face of the main bearing journal of the crankshaft and the crankshaft drive sprocket. The camshaft drive sprockets and Morse chain were narrower (¹³⁄₃₂in) than stock two-barrel 289ci engine items, which allowed space for the counterweight without any other engine components needing to be altered. The camshaft drive sprocket on the crankshaft was unique to the Hi-Performance 289; it was shorter than the stock 289ci item, and had a hole in it to take a pin that located the supplementary counterweight.

The ¹³⁄₃₂in Morse chains and nylon/aluminium camshaft drive sprockets met all of Ford's durability requirements, but wore far too quickly in stock road use – to the point that these engines had retarded camshaft and ignition timing by the 25,000 mile mark. The ignition timing could be easily adjusted, but the camshaft timing couldn't without replacing the chain. When new the camshaft chain and sprockets were quite difficult to fit onto the crankshaft and camshaft. Around the 25,000 mile mark it was common for there to be a good ¼in deflection when checked using Ford's recommended method. This didn't tend to result in a major loss of power, despite the slackness in the chain. The result was more of a gradual power loss, which wasn't really noticeable. By 100,000 miles the chains and sprockets would be well worn and need to be replaced, yet there was no history of failure, even at this high mileage. The engines that did fail only did so after the nylon teeth had actually broken off. Early sprockets maintaining the basic tooth form size were cast iron rather than nylon/aluminium, and these would suffer indentation marks. The ¹³⁄₃₂in chain remained the same throughout production of the Hi-Performance 289, which wore equally irrespective of sprocket type.

The oil pump, pickup and oil pump driveshaft fitted to all Hi-Performance

289 engines were standard production components.

Ford fitted a four-barrel vacuum secondary 4100 Series Autolite carburettor rated at 480 CFM to a cast iron four-barrel inlet manifold. The venturi/choke diameters were 1.120in, and the inlet manifold was more or less the same in configuration and internal passageway size as the two-barrel carburettor item, but with a four-barrel carburettor placement. These particular 4100 carburettors were fitted with a manual choke as opposed to an automatic one, making them unique to these engines.

The Hi-Performance 289 was an out-and-out performance engine, not renowned for its fuel economy. It characteristically did about 12-13mpg on average. By comparison, the 221ci would return about 19mpg, the 260ci about 18mpg, the 289ci-2V about 16mpg, and the 289ci-4V about 15mpg. These figures are based on manual transmission and would be on average about 1mpg less for automatic.

Other unique features of the Hi-Performance 289 engine included specially designed, free-flowing cast iron exhaust manifolds, a FoMoCo dual-point distributor without vacuum advance (1963-1964), and an Autolite (1965-1967). A vacuum advance canister was fitted until June 1963, but

it wasn't operative: it was fitted because it located the distributor cap. From June the vaccum canister was deleted.

The Hi-Performance 289 clutch was heavy-duty compared to stock. The springs in the centre of the clutch disc/clutch plate and the pressure plate/clutch cover assembly were much stronger than stock, making the clutch action heavy: it required quite a lot of foot pressure to disengage the clutch.

Some of the last Hi-Performance 289 engines to be produced went to California fitted with a Thermactor emission control system to comply with the engine pollution regulations there. Fourteen engines with this specification were made, and each retained the 4100 carburettor.

The Hi-Performance 289 petrol pump differed from standard in that it had a different actuating arm and an extra spring for better high rpm control of the arm, and therefore a more consistent high rpm output.

The six-vane water pump fitted to Hi-Performance 289 engines had a 4in diameter compared to the 4¾in diameter of stock 221ci, 260ci and 289ci items, which reduced the prospect of cavitation at high rpm. In August 1964 the stock 289ci water pump impeller diameter was reduced to 4in, and the vane count increased to eight.

In June 1965 the aluminium water pump on all 289ci engines was replaced by a cast iron item with pressed steel backing plates. The timing chain cover behind the water pump remained aluminium. The change was due to the cavitation erosion of the aluminium timing chain cover by the anti-freeze mix being used and the proportions it was being mixed at. The anti-freeze Ford used at the time contained arsenic, and the recommended anti-freeze mix was highly corrosive; it was an auto-industry wide issue with engines that had aluminium pumps and timing chain covers. Ford later developed its own much less corrosive product with a 50/50 anti-freeze to water mix. Although the new water pump was much heavier than the previous aluminium version, the steel backing plate between the pump and the timing chain cover was a much more robust configuration, and there were no further erosion problems. The projected revolution ranges of the engines meant a more efficient fan, which drew more air through the radiator, was fitted – unique to this engine application.

The Hi-Performance 289 engine was used in a wide range of applications, from Ford Mustangs, Fairlanes, Mercury Comets and AC Cobras, with best estimates placing the total number made at about 24,000.

Chapter 3
255ci Indianapolis 500 pushrod engine of 1963

The 1963 Indianapolis 500 engine project came about after Colin Chapman of Lotus observed the success Jack Brabham had at Indy in 1962 with a rear engine Cooper-Climax Formula One car fitted with a 165ci/2.7-litre FPF Coventry Climax engine. This engine was a bored and stroked version of the 153ci/2.5-litre FPF Formula One unit, as used by Jack Brabham to win the 1959 and 1960 World Championships for Cooper, specially built for the Indianaoplis race with about 255bhp.

For further information on the FPF 2.5- and 2.7-litre engine, and the Formula One Coventry Climax 91.5ci/1.5-litre FWMV engine, as used in the Lotus 25 and mentioned later in this chapter, consult *Coventry Climax Racing Engines – The Definitive Development History* written by Des Hammill and published by Veloce Publishing: the book is available from specialist motoring book shops or direct from www.velocebooks.com/ www.veloce.co.uk.

Soon after the Cooper car effort Colin Chapman proposed to Ford management a new car built for use at Indianapolis that would take a small block Ford V8 engine. Ford saw an opportunity to advertise the similarity between a 255ci/4.2-litre Indanapolis racing engine and its production 260ci V8 being used in Ford Fairlane and Mercury Meteor cars. The 260ci version of the original 221ci small block engine was well suited to the application, being around the same capacity as the requirement for the Indianapolis 500.

When it comes to specialised versions of these engines used for the Indianapolis 500 in 1963, 1964 and 1965, it's necessary to be aware that Ford management was primarily focused on winning this one race for advertising purposes. In the lead-up to the event it was a case of get the job done by whatever means, but as soon as the race was won, the programme was cancelled and the engineers involved went on to other work.

It's also essential to understand that the Engine and Foundry Division completed work for other divisions of the Ford Motor Company. It received orders for engines from various divisions within the company, such as Ford Division, for example, and each engine project would be funded by the division that ordered it. In the case of the Indianapolis 500 engine project, once the race had been won, it was mission accomplished as far as the particular division of the Ford Motor Company funding it was concerned, and strict financial guidelines applied at all times.

Jacques Passino, Homer Perry and Bill Himphrey were the coordinators of Ford Division, which provided the funding to design and develop an engine for the 1963 Indy 500 Lotus car. The engine project was assigned to the

Advanced Engine Department of the Engine and Foundry Division, and given the code AX230. Within this engineering environment each Advanced Engine project was given a sequential number for identification purposes – 'AX' indicated 'Advanced Experimental' project.

In 1962, the engineers in Advanced Engineering planned to use a double overhead camshaft (DOHC) setup for the 1963 Indianapolis racing engine. The code AX227 had even been assigned before they were over-ruled by upper-management and directed to execute a derivative of the basic 260ci pushrod engine coded AX230 instead. The decision was based on the potential advertising opportunity it might afford – it came from those funding the project and therefore having the say. Stock production cars were fitted with a pushrod engine and not a double overhead camshaft engine, so going too specialised would reduce the impact of a win for advertising purposes. So for the time being, project code AX227 was for administrative use only, and the AX230 pushrod engine with its higher code number was introduced first.

The Advanced Engine Department was managed by Bill Gay. The engineers on this project were Joe Macura, Ed Pinkerton, Dick Chen, Ralph Rays and Bill Gelgota, and there were dozens of analysis, drafting, material procurement, engine build-up and inspection staff involved.

All of the work was carried out in the Engine & Electrical Engineering (EEE), or 'the Triple-E building' as the workers called it, at the Ford Engine Centre in Dearborn, adjacent to the Henry Ford museum. In the Dynamometer Department Bill Barr was the engine test engineer, and Bill Phillips and Chuck Teezar were the

dynamometer operators. All of the development testing was done on a GE engine dynamometer that Ford purchased at the end of 1962, and it was capable of taking an engine turning up to 8000rpm.

The 1963 Indy engine project was analysed and designed between June and August 1962. It involved three series of engine. Series I was a modified production all cast iron 260ci engine. Five were made, and they were coded AX192. Series II featured aluminium block and cylinder heads, produced to the final design for general testing and inlet and exhaust manifold design and development verification work. Seven units were produced under code AX195. Finally, Series III was the complete final race design. Nine were made under code AX230, one of which was actually raced. The original 260ci engine stroke of 2.870in was retained, as was the connecting rod centre-to-centre distance length of 5.155in, giving the engine a 1.78:1 connecting rod to stroke ratio.

The 1963 project progressed very well. The race engines were tested up to the 8000rpm limit of the dynamometer, which was deemed high enough to ensure reliability, and there were few engine failures during testing. The blocks, cylinder heads, crankshafts, pistons, connecting rods and valve train components were all very robustly designed to go the required distance, and then some. With the electronic limiting disconnected from the dynamometer, 8500rpm was tested on a couple of occasions. The engine's maximum power output of 375bhp was achieved at 7200rpm.

The largest amount of testing time throughout the project was allotted to setting up the four 58mm, twin-barrel, down-draught Weber carburettors. These carburettors were so large for

this capacity engine that accurately calibrating them engrossed several Ford engineers, as well as a Mr Vito from Weber in Italy for the final month and a half until the May 30th race. Mr Vito bought a mass of jetting with him from Italy, and systematically went through every combination. In the end he managed to make the engine run correctly. Bearing in mind that the engine was turning high rpm throughout its application and the carburettors were sized accordingly, low rpm performance was not startling.

Although Ford engineers tried Hilborn fuel injection on these engines, and achieved more power from the engine with methanol, it was specified that carburettors had to be used if possible. Road-going versions of the engine used carburettors, and Ford wanted its customers to know that the race engine at Indianapolis used them too, even though the Weber carburettors in question were nothing like the stock FoMoCo items, except for the fixed choke principle. Ford used Hilborn fuel injection components sourced from Hilborn Fuel Injection Engineering, but produced its own inlet manifold assemblies.

Ford Division upper-management had stressed to the engineers the need for absolute reliability, and this pushrod version of the basic 260ci engine, downsized to 255ci via a reduced bore, had the best of everything in it technically, with all aspects of high performance taken to the logical conclusion. It was powerful and reliable. Ford and Lotus were very unlucky indeed not to have won at Indianapolis in 1963 when using it for the first time. In fact, had race officials black-flagged cars that were dropping oil on the track as they should have, Jim Clark driving his Lotus-Ford would certainly have won the race.

The Indianapolis 500 was clouded in controversy that year because of the 'oil dropping' incident. Colin Chapman of Lotus was particularly scathing of the Indianapolis race officials and why Lotus came second as opposed to first. At the drivers' briefing before the start of 1963 event all competitors were told that any car dropping oil would immediately be black-flagged. The lead car was clearly seen dropping oil late in the race; and lots of it. Rather than be black-flagged, it was allowed to continue dropping oil, and this meant the cars behind it had to slow down to avoid sliding or losing control and crashing into the wall. As this was happening, Colin Chapman confidently predicted that the car would run out of oil and the engine would blow-up, allowing a Lotus to take the lead and win. What he didn't realise however, was that these cars carried a massive amount of oil, and the car went on to win the race.

A furious Colin Chapman was very vocal in accusing the Americans of cheating. He realised there and then that they would do virtually anything to stop a Lotus car winning their race. This only made Chapman more determined to succeed, which of course he did. He claimed that the US 'Roadsters' were "great piles of junk" and about 20-30 years out of date technology-wise – comments not well received in some quarters.

In a way it was fortunate that Ford didn't win at this first attempt in 1963. If it had, its four valve per cylinder, DOHC V8 engine, that would power winning cars on several occasions, may not have been made. In fact, it can be said with absolute certainty that this DOHC engine would not have been introduced, because one Indianapolis 500 win was all that Ford required.

With the help of the Ford

Motor Company, Colin Chapman of Lotus Cars ultimately revolutionised Indianapolis-type racing in the mid-1960s into what it is today. However, the credit for starting the rear engine trend at Indianapolis clearly goes to Charles and John Cooper, and Jack Brabham, along with Leonard Lee and Walter Hassan of Coventry Climax, who supplied the special 2.7-litre FPF engine. They took a rear-engined Cooper Formula One-type racing car to Indy in 1961 and did very well with it.

SAE PAPER 818A

The following is the SAE paper written by Bill Gay following the 1963 Indianapolis 500. He explains the reasons Ford undertook the project, its objectives, and covers the technical detail of the engine.

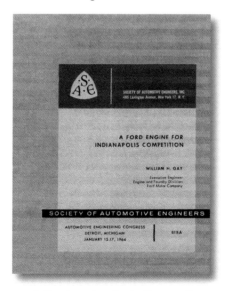

A Ford engine for Indianapolis Competition.

By Mr W H Gay - Executive Engineer of the Ford Motor Company

Engine and Foundry Division of the Ford Motor Company – Automotive Engineering Congress 1964

Introduction

The decision of the Ford motor Company to participate in competitive events was based on sound technical reasons associated with the demands of today's market. The market today is far more sophisticated that it was prior to World War II. Buyer demands of that earlier period were more easily satisfied. There was comparatively little demand for a variety of choices in a product, or for frequent changes to the product. Today's buyers on the other hand demand variety and change in unprecedented amounts, and they expect, as they have a right to, that whatever they select has been thoroughly tested and proven. The job of designing and developing engines for today's passenger car market requires the engineer to use every means at his disposal to find every shortcoming in an engine in the shortest possible time. Today, our engineers can test engines in the full range of competitive events as well as in the conventional manner. These competitive events provide rugged accelerated test conditions not available on the highway and proving ground, and cover a range of performance evaluation on six fronts:

1 – Stock car racing
2 – Road rallies
3 – Economy runs
4 – Drag events
5 – Road racing
6 – Indianapolis competition

Historically, the race track has been known to the engineer for its all-out demands on engines. Since the stakes for the race driver are high, and his competitive instinct is intense, he makes greater demands on an engine that can be expected of the proving ground driver. Like-wise, the challenge to win

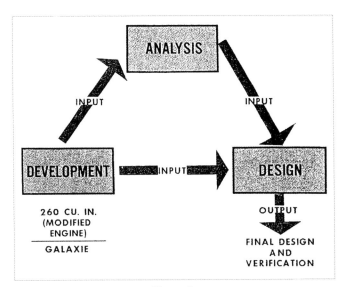

Figure 1.

OBJECTIVES

1. COMPLETE THE RACE IN ONLY ONE PIT STOP

2. CARRY AND CONSUME A TOTAL OF ONLY 400gal OF FUEL (THIS PRECLUDED THE USE OF EXOTIC FUELS INVOLVING A PENALTY OF 800gal FUEL LOAD)

3. CARRY ONLY 24gal OF OIL INSTEAD OF THE NORMAL 80gal

4. USE CARBURETION IN PLACE OF FUEL INJECTION

5. LIMIT COMPLETE INSTALLED ENGINE WEIGHT TO 350lb/160kg

6. USE AUTOMOTIVE BATTERY IGNITION AND A DISTRIBUTOR INSTEAD OF A MAGNETO

7. DEVELOP A MINIMUM OF 325 DEPENDABLE HORSEPOWER FROM 255 CU. IN.

Figure 2.

in open competitive events of all kinds stimulates engineering imagination and ability, and racing provides our engine engineers unparalleled opportunities to demonstrate their high degree of engineering achievement. The Advanced Engine Engineering Department of Ford's Engine and Foundry Division eagerly accepted the Indianapolis assignment and looked forward to solving the many technical problems we knew it would present. The determination to qualify, the hope to finish the race, and the possibility of winning the Indianapolis 500 Mile Classic presented a strong challenge to our engineering team. This paper describes in some detail the engineering approach to, and the solution of the technical problems encountered in adapting a production pushrod engine for Indianapolis competition.

Objectives

Since the assignment was given to us some time after the 1962 race, there was not much time available to reach our objectives. Hardly any time could be allocated for alternative trials or explorations. We had to adhere to, and make the most of, whatever key decisions were made along the way without appeals or reversals. First of all, and most important, the 260ci small block Ford production engine used in the Ford Fairlane 500, Ford Falcon, and Mercury Comet cars was selected as most suited to readily meet the Indianapolis displacement limit, which is 4.2 litres or 256.284ci (cubic inches). A slight reduction in the displacement of our production engine would permit us to meet this race entry regulation. The use of the 260ci engine would eliminate the need for the usual preliminary design work that precedes construction of a new engine. Design did not precede development. Instead, performance data was generated and durability problems raised from existing prototype engines. They were studied in the light of sound engineering judgement based on past experience, and subjected to strict computer analysis, which in co-ordination with progressive development, produced the final design.

Construction of the racing car chassis was the responsibility of Colin Chapman of Lotus reputation. On the basis of the projected specifications of his car design, we jointly listed what should be expected from the engines (see Figure 2).

This list was to be subjected to verification and considerable revisions in step with our progress. We set up the following programme timing (see Figure 3):

1 – Survey the Indianapolis track during August of 1962.
2 – Investigate the maximum horsepower capabilities of our production 260ci engine by September 1962, and compare our performance with the measured output of a purchased Offenhauser engine.
3 – Conduct vehicle performance tests of a Lotus 25 Formula One car with a known Coventry Climax 1.5-litre FWMV engine during October 1962.
4 – Duplicate the production 260ci engine in aluminium and resolve any basic weight or high speed durability problems by November 1st 1962.
5 – Obtain competitive vehicle data to

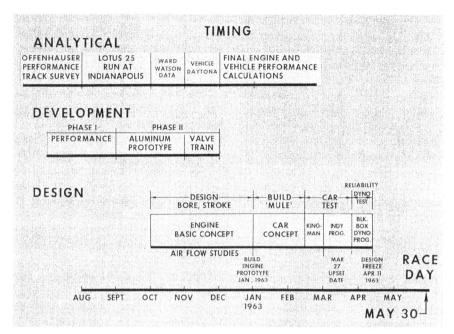

Figure 3.

verify our performance calculations. and supply analytical results for final engine design and car concept by November 1962.

6 – Complete basic engines tests at Daytona by December 1962.

7 – Design, build and test a new engine and car concept prior to our April 1963 'upset date.'

Development (Phase 1)

While we were having 260ci engine parts modified, and the Indianapolis track survey was being completed, we conducted performance tests of the Offenhauser engine on a dynamometer (see Figure 4). The Offenhauser engine is a very large capacity four cylinder, in-line, double overhead camshaft racing engine employing a gear train camshaft drive and an exceptionally large induction system specifically designed for fuel injection of methanol and nitro-methane fuel. It contains four valves per cylinder. Each bore is 4.281in/108.7mm in diameter, and the

stroke is 4.375in/120.6mm. It has a compression ratio of 14.95:1, and has been tailored to the requirements of the Indianapolis speedway by camshaft phasing and the most advantageous locating of its torque peak.

The 'Awful Offy' proved to be awfully good on our dynamometer by developing 401bhp at 6000rpm and a torque of 378lb-ft at 5000rpm. It is worth noting that the maximum brake mean effective pressure (bmep) of this engine on methanol fuel is 227psi. Since the Offenhauser engine was calibrated to burn methanol fuel, only the baseline was established with this fuel. All the data needed for our computer programme was extracted from this engine, and a complete survey was carried out, including volumetric efficiency, which showed results close to

100% for several speeds. Concurrently we proceeded to run evaluation tests of our modified 260ci engine. The following changes had been incorporated:

1 – Four dual-throat 46mm diameter down-draught Weber carburettors were installed.

2 – The intake and exhaust ports and the valves were modified on the basis of static air flow bench studies.

3 – The combustion chamber was revised by relocating the sparkplug and providing a domed piston crown with provision for a three-path flame travel. The resultant compression ratio was 12.5:1.

4 – The valve train was revised by adding light weight mechanical tappets, a teflon pushrod guide, dual valve springs, an aluminium valve spring retainer, screw-in rocker arm stud, hollow valves, and a camshaft with a opening factor of 0.00038in/0.01011mm per 0.4 of a degree of camshaft rotation.

This engine easily surpassed our objective of 325bhp, but that was on gasoline and the results were not directly comparable to those of the Offenhauser engine that was

Figure 4. Offenhauser engine.

tailored to methanol. This led us into the controversial subject of racing fuels. It is probably safe to say that every blend of fuel capable of being ignited by a spark has been used. The blends of racing fuel that have proved best are aviation gasoline/petrol, benzol acetone, methyl alcohol, ethyl alcohol, isopropyl alcohol, and butyl alcohol. Other additive agents such as nitro-compounds, water, organic nitrates, peroxides, tetraethyl lead, ether, and explosive elements have been used. However, the air/fuel ratio and heating value in British Thermal Units (btu) per pound of fuel are the key to power output and possible advantage. The high specific gravity and the low stoichiometric ratio of exotic fuels presented a disadvantage to us because we wanted to consume only 400 gallons of fuel in the whole course of the race. We experimented with several fuels to study their pre-ignition tendencies, octane limited effect, and latent heat of vaporization against volumetric efficiency; we also mixed several nitro-parafins. By making several runs on methanol we were able to compare our engine with the Offenhauser (see Figure 5). This data spelled out the distinct advantage of the Offenhauser engine and seemed to substantiate our previous analytical study. This study had indicated that because of the short straightaways (between the corners at Indianapolis), torque wins at Indianapolis.

In summary, our data indicated a performance improvement of 10-12% by substituting methanol for gasoline/petrol. Upon adding nitro-methane to methanol we obtained data which showed an improvement of 1/3 of 1% increase in indicated power for each percent of nitro-methane added. Consequently, a 20% improvement in horsepower was possible with a mixture

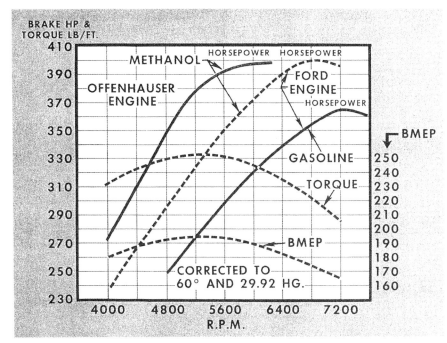

Figure 5. Performance comparison.

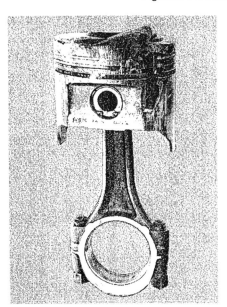

Figure 6. Burnt piston from the use of nitro-methane in methanol.

of 30% nitro-methane in methanol. This involved a penalty of 2½ to 3 times the gasoline/petrol consumption, providing of course that the engine

could tolerate this oxygen-laden fuel reliably. Figure 6 concludes our fuel studies, and reinforces our decision to use gasoline/petrol as a dependable low-consumption fuel and to shun all exotic additives.

Analytical

It became clear that the original objective of 325bhp on gasoline/petrol would at best produce an optimum lap speed of only 146mph. 365bhp on gasoline/petrol would make possible 150.50mph. 400bhp on methanol would make possible 153mph. Finally, 425bhp on gasoline/petrol could achieve a 155mph lap speed. We now had a driver pattern and a horsepower rating that indicated we should go at least 150mph. The accuracy of this last figure would be proven later in the programme when confirmation of our calculations would be checked by car testing in March 1963 at Kingman, Arizona and the Indianapolis Speedway.

FUEL	H.P.	N/V	AVG. TURN SPEED	RPM	LAP SPEED (MPH)
GASOLINE	325*	39.7	140	7200	146
GAS	350	40	141	7500	149
GAS	365	39	141	7500	150.5
MET	400	38	141	7200	153
GAS	425	42	142	8000	155

Figure 7. Calculated Lotus-Ford lap speeds
(*program objective).

Figure 8. Ford-Lotus transistorized ignition system.

Development (Phase 2)

Further work with a Ford engine was required to verify objectives not associated with lap speed. Duplicates of the 260ci engines with aluminium cylinder block and cylinder heads were built for this work. Additional modifications, such as adapting fuel injection and reducing the displacement to the track regulations, were incorporated (meaning all engines used so far were 260ci and not 255ci). These engines, whether using carburettors with gasoline/petrol or fuel injection with methanol, duplicated the power output of the original modified all cast iron production 260ci engine. The light weight 255ci engine was installed in a 1962 Galaxie, and in November the car was shipped to Daytona Speedway to assess variables such as engine crankcase breathing, cooling, starting, battery size and ignition. Four days and 435 miles of track testing revealed that the engine when equipped with Hilborn fuel injection and running on methanol was 8.1mph faster than the engine on carburettors and using gasoline/petrol. That's 154.8mph on methanol and 146.7mph on gasoline/petrol, although this was achieved at a considerable sacrifice in fuel economy, which

dropped from 6.41mpg to 2.22mpg on methanol. However, carburettors larger than the dual-throat 46mm diameter Webers were on order, and it was expected that they would narrow down the performance difference quite decisively. The fuel economy obtained would bear out our initial analytical study. On this basis the decision to 'go gasoline' was reaffirmed for a second time. All crankcase breathing, cooling issues, and generator and battery sizes were selected.

Ignition problems were solved by the use of a new, special transistorized system of a breakerless-type based on a variable reluctance principle. This design employs a concentric permanent magnet and coil with a toothed rotor which varies the reluctance of the magnetic circuit as it rotates, and thereby generates a voltage waveform in the coil. It was decided for reliability reasons to operate at a fixed timing of 51 degrees before top dead centre at 1000rpm. It was mentioned earlier that we modified our combustion chamber for a three-path flame front for best breathing performance, however this combustion chamber design required a high amount of spark advance (ignition

timing) and thereby caused a starting problem in the vehicle at Daytona. This problem was resolved by retarding the spark advance (ignition timing) 30 degrees during the cranking and engine starting cycle by means of a switch positioned between the distributor and the amplifier. This switch momentarily reverses the output from the magnetic circuit, and the result is approximately 20 degrees of spark advance (ignition timing) for starting purposes.

Two problems that occurred during dynamometer testing were confirmed on the aluminium engine during car testing at Daytona: valve train limitations and head gasket problems.

Design Components

Based on our analytical and development programme, design modifications affecting practically every component were required in order to achieve more than twice the power of the original 260ci engine with a 25% reduction in total weight. In spite of these modifications, the Indianapolis engine retains a remarkable degree of resemblance to the production engine. A description of the design modifications of the major engine components follows:

1 – The bore size was reduced from the stock 3.800in/96.5mm to 3.760in/95.4mm to give 255ci displacement.

2 – The front flange of the block was modified to be able to take cases for the gear-driven camshaft, water pump, distributor and dry-sump oil pumps.

3 – The block deck thickness was increased by 50% to 0.640in/16.2mm.

4 – All bolt bosses were made longer to obtain a minimum of two times the diameter of thread engagement.

5 – The main cap mounting faces (block main cap register) were extended to accommodate four-bolt nodular iron main bearing caps, except the rearmost one, which remained a two-bolt (main cap was nodular iron).

6 – Modification to the block deck and side of the block permitted the use of two additional studs per cylinder (effective six instead of four).

7 – Provision was made for installing dry cast iron liners with a light press fit into the block of 0.001-0.002in/0.0254-0.0508mm.

8 – In order to seal the combustion gases, a groove was machined in the top of the liner flange for a metal 'O'-ring gasket, which consists of 5 laminated steel discs in a flanged steel casing resembling an 'O'-ring. With cylinder head and block deck surfaces sealed, allowance was made for two oil drain-back holes and one oil pressure hole to take oil to the rocker shafts and rocker arms at the front of the block, also two water transfer holes and one oil drain-back hole at the rear of the block. These holes were sealed with conventional rubber 'O'-rings. The 'O'-ring around each cylinder bears the whole concentrated load from the cylinder head studs, and a 0.010-0.015in/0.25-0.375mm air gap is created between the faces of the cylinder block deck and cylinder head facing surface, as shown in Figure 9.

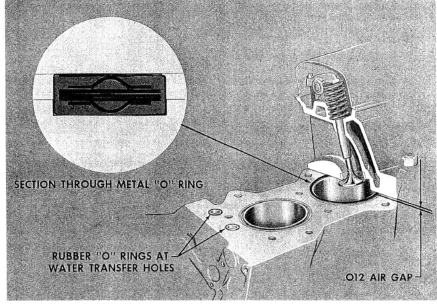

Figure 9. Cylinder head gasket design.

The cylinder heads, like the block, were sand-cast in aluminium from reworked experimental 260ci engine patterns. They feature:

1 – Aluminium bronze valve guides, hardened steel valve seat inserts, steel valve spring seat bases.

2 – Revised water jackets that redirect the water outlet from the intake manifold face to the front of the cylinder head, and an added boss to supply oil under pressure to the overhead valve gear.

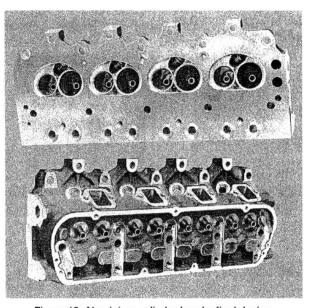

Figure 10. Aluminium cylinder heads; final design.

3 – Four bosses added to the exhaust side of the cylinder head, and four studs added on the intake side of the cylinders to improve gasket sealing.

4 – Enlarged intake and exhaust ports with modification of the combustion chamber.

The crankshaft was made out of 4136 steel with revised counterweighting. For space considerations we added a fifth counterweight to the crankshaft to eliminate the need for external balance. The over-plated copper-lead production bearings were retained. The connecting rod crank journals (crank pins) and main bearing journals were cross-drilled to meet the needs of high-speed lubrication. To reduce counterweighting requirements the crank pins were drilled from both sides and plugged with steel cup plugs backed with swaged steel pins.

Chapter 4

Shelby American Hi-Performance 289ci racing engines 1963-1967

Shelby American was without a doubt at the forefront of the development and racing use of the Hi-Performance 289ci from when the engines first became available for racing purposes in its AC Cobra sports cars. What follows is Shelby American's prescription for the modification of these engines, from their introduction in early 1963 to the end of 1965, before Ford had made any special racing parts.

The emphasis of the original 221ci engine lay firmly on designing a light weight, compact unit commensurate with standard economical road use. There were certainly no intentions of use for racing purposes. However, as mentioned earlier, less than six months into production, Carroll Shelby expressed an interest in a high-powered

version for his AC Ace sports car project, and Ford began performance development to specifically comply with his wishes. This version of the 260ci engine was completed in January 1962, and became known as the Hi-Performance 260.

There were between six and eight Hi-Performance 260ci engines intended for use by Shelby American in racing applications, which were stripped down and rebuilt with several differences.

The engine builders at Shelby American considered the connecting rod bolts too small for high rpm use, so these were replaced with $^{11}/_{32}$in high strength aftermarket versions. It wasn't simply a matter of substituting the original bolts with stronger items, though. To achieve this Shelby

American also had to re-machine the connecting rods. In addition, the standard Ford cast pistons were replaced with Forged True raised, top forged items designed for higher output racing engines.

The best of these race-prepared Hi-Performance 260 engines developed in the vicinity of 290-335bhp, depending on the level of modification. They featured several induction systems, including: Holley four-barrel carburettor and aluminium high rise inlet manifold; four side-draught Weber carburettors; many different camshafts from Engle or Iskenderian; dual contra-wound coil valve springs; and related aftermarket valve train components, such as steel turned valve spring retainers and split locks.

The Hi-Performance 260 engine wasn't used for racing purposes after the introduction of the Hi-Performance 289. This very limited production Hi-Performance 260 engine was without a doubt the forerunner to the production Hi-Performance 289 engines of 1963-1967.

Shelby American already had a year's worth of experience with the small block Ford V8 engine when the greater specification Hi-Performance 289 became available in February 1963. This engine was inherently better than the Hi-Performance 260, what with its stronger connecting rods, pistons and crankshaft. When the engine was introduced engineer Buck Yearbeck from Ford Engine Engineering claimed publicly that it was capable of 7000rpm, which was quite correct in that it could take this sort of treatment for a reasonable amount of time.

The 1963-1965 Hi-Performance 289 Shelby American racing engines retained the use of many stock Ford parts. In fact, a remarkable number of stock Ford parts gave very good service in racing. The drivers were told that the Shelby American-built engines were good for 7000rpm, and to avoid turning them more than that. Most drivers understood this and did their best to comply; it was in their interest to follow such advice because you can't win a race if you over-rev the engine and it fails. Reliability of these engines was based on very frequent component replacement within reasonable usage time scales; the engines were being used by the top drivers of the day, so had to be right or there would be no chance of winning races.

There wasn't a major engine development programme – to discover everything there was to know about these engines and formulate a set process of rebuilding them for racing purposes – at Shelby American as such. It was more of a progressive development, with small steps being taken by a range of very talented engine builders. The incremental changes were made so as not to compromise the all-important reliability. Each engine builder who came to work at Shelby American tended to bring various ideas with them, and this was key to the success of the operation. The main engine builders, Cecil Bowman, Jack Hoare, 'Ole' Olsen and Jim O'Leary, were encouraged to compete against each other to see who could build the best engine.

The Hi-Performance 289 engines Shelby American used for drag racing purposes were turned to 8000rpm. This higher rpm figure was achievable without compromising reliability due to the inherent low milage application – certainly nothing like the road racing engines.

Stock valve springs were initially used for racing (singles with a flat wound damper inside), but they were not used for long. The engine builders preferred to use dual coils, and these single versions were not considered to have enough tension for the rpm. As a result, aftermarket dual contra-wound coil springs were used instead, usually sourced from Sig Erson. The objective was to attain 350lb of 'over the nose' valve spring pressure irrespective of the valve lift, and have in the vicinity of 130-150lb of seated pressure. Stock Hi-Performance 289 valve spring retainers and split locks were used for racing purposes. These proved reliable, but when Shelby American began using dual valves of varying sizes the spring retainers didn't necessarily fit, so aftermarket steel items were fitted.

The stock timing chain and iron sprockets were used exclusively in these early years, and never changed over to the nylon toothed/aluminium camshaft drive sprocket. The engine builders used to drill a number of extra holes in the iron sprockets for camshaft indexing, and it was felt that the aluminium sprocket wasn't suitable for this. When a camshaft was 'timed in' during assembly, the original dowel hole in the sprocket very often wasn't in the right place to obtain suitable camshaft timing, so the engine builders would pick another tooth and drill another hole further round from the original, to either advance or retard the camshaft as was required. The engineers became skilled at estimating the correct position on the pitch circle diameter where the 'new' hole should be placed.

All blocks were checked for main bearing tunnel size and alignment using a high-tensile steel precision ground mandrel of the right size. Most blocks were correct as machined; Ford being well noted for its very accurate machining capability, with only one or two out of hundreds being less than ideal. None of the Shelby American engine builders liked the idea of align-honing the main bearing tunnel bores because even a small reduction in the centre-to-centre distance between the crankshaft and camshaft caused an undesirable slackening of the timing chain.

The stock Hi-Performance 289 cast pistons were used in nearly all instances during 1963-1965, with a very low in service failure rate. They looked exactly the same as the standard 289ci engine pistons, but differed in that they were made from high silicon content material, making the aluminium what is termed hypereutectic. The valve reliefs were made deeper and slightly larger in diameter to match the larger $1\frac{7}{8}$in inlet and $1\frac{5}{8}$in exhaust valves fitted into the Hi-Performance 289 cylinder heads.

Other than this, the relief valves were as manufactured by Ford.

In most cases the pistons were replaced at each engine rebuild, usually following 4-6 hours of racing. Engines were sometimes stripped down before this time for a variety of reasons, and pistons would be reused if they passed the crack testing and measurement criteria and procedure. If the skirts were worn from standard, or there were non-typical wear marks on them, or the top compression ring groove was not to original size, they would be replaced.

These stock pistons featured on racing engines with an average 0.004in piston to bore clearance. Despite these engines being revved to a maximum of 7000rpm throughout races, there were very few piston failures, even when 400bhp was being extracted, as in the case of the four down-draught Weber equipped units. The press-in fit of the gudgeon pins into the little end of the connecting rod was maintained. Chrome plated top compression rings were initially fitted, but moly rings started to be used in 1964. This change eventually became permanent, due to a slight gain in power.

Hi-Performance 289 engines had either flat-top or raised-top pistons, and Shelby American modified cylinder heads, as used 1963-1965, ran best in conjunction with flat-top pistons; they did not respond to raised-top versions. The two valve reliefs below the valves were increased in diameter and depth to offer clearance for the larger valves fitted, which made the pistons left or right cylinder bank specific. Compression ratios used in 1963-1965 with stock flat-top pistons and modified Hi-Performance 289ci stock cylinder heads were on average 10.0:1 to perhaps 10.5:1 with higher octane Sunoco 260 gasoline. This fuel's octane

rating of 107 RON and 100 MON was higher than technically required, but it was readily available in the USA, consistent in quality, and had a very high Tetraeythl lead content of 3-4g plus per gallon.

Stock Hi-Performance 289ci connecting rods were used, but with slightly larger diameter ($^{13}/_{32}$in) 427ci FE engine connecting rod bolts fitted to them. This came from the Shelby American engine builders' desire to use the largest and strongest bolt available. The thinking at the time was that the slightly larger diameter bolts from the 427ci racing engine would offer superior clamping power, not that the original $^3/_8$in bolts weren't good enough. Hi-Performance connecting rods were generally replaced after two major road races, which essentially meant (as with the pistons) every 4-6 racing hours, although a car entered in a 12-hour race would obviously keep the same connecting rods for the whole event. A set of connecting rods that endured a 12-hour race, for example, would certainly never be used again.

Stock bore blocks were used exclusively, and when the bores were worn by 0.002in the block was replaced. Depending on the conditions the engine was being used under (dust and dirt was the problem), this meant an average service life of 8-12 racing hours. The blocks were very reliable overall, and didn't develop cracks or suffer main cap to block surface fretting within this usage time frame.

The stock Ford main cap and cylinder head bolts were initially used without problem, but in 1965 some of the engine builders began to use more torque on the cylinder head bolts than recommended – taking the bolts past their elastic limit. The standard bolts were substituted with Allen headed cap screws because of their proven

uniform material quality and heat-treatment. More Ford involvement later in 1965 meant a return to the use of its bolts as the company wanted these engines to be all Ford. Unfortunately, when the new Ford supplied bolts were introduced there was a spate of cylinder head gasket failures during races, and the likely cause was traced to the Ford bolts not being to specification heat treatment/hardness/toughness. At this point Shelby American engine builders reverted to Allen headed cap screws. It could have been just a bad batch of Ford bolts Shelby American received, but it wouldn't take a chance on them again. Studs and nuts were also used from time to time.

The Hi-Performance crankshaft, supplementary counterweight and camshaft drive sprocket were trouble-free, as was the standard Ford Hi-Performance 289ci flywheel. Cobras and Mustangs used the stock iron flywheel, while other engine installations, such as rear engine sports cars, required the use of a special steel flywheel and twin plate clutch systems. There were some crankshaft damper failures in longer races, though. The outer ring of the damper would move, and if there were any balancing holes in the outer rim the engine would go out of balance and start to vibrate. The rings never came off the damper, they just moved on the elastomeric material. The solution for distance racing was to use only crankshaft dampers without balance correction holes in the ring; ensuring that no holes were drilled in the ring when the engine assembly was checked for balance. Then, if the ring was to move in a race, it wouldn't affect the engine. It would mean that the ignition timing marks would become out of place, but this wasn't such an issue because the damper would be replaced at the next engine rebuild.

Stock Ford Hi-Performance 289ci main, big end and camshaft bearings were initially used, but the mains and big ends were changed to Federal Mogul or Clevitte. Crankshaft main bearing journals supplied by Federal Mogul and Clevitte were grooved for 360 degree connecting rod oiling, while the stock Ford Hi-Performance 289ci ones were not. These two companies also supplied bearings in two sizes, for selective fit. The mains and big ends tended to be run with 0.0025-0.003in clearances.

The standard oil pump was used, but with the housing adjusted to reduce the end float to the 0.002in minimum. This minimised pumping losses within the pump itself. The relief valve spring was packed with a 0.250in spacer, which increased the oil pressure to 65-70psi on average. The stock oil pickup arrangement was fitted, but was braced to prevent the pipe and gauze faced pickup from falling off due to vibration.

Stock oil shaft drives were fitted, very often with two retaining clips. The clips stopped the oil shaft lifting with the distributor, if it was removed, and also prevented the end of the shaft coming out of the oil pump and falling into the sump, which would necessitate a partial engine strip down; removing the sump to retrieve it. These drives were replaced at every engine rebuild and never failed – it took debris in the Gerotor or an oil pump seizure to twist the hexagon shaft into a spiral.

A range of camshafts were used on these engines, the vast majority of which were the flat tappet-type as opposed to roller lifter. The camshafts were sourced from Engle, Sig Erson, Racer Brown and Iskenderian. All manner of camshafts were tried in an effort to improve the power output of these engines – lifts of up to 0.560in were tried, although 0.500in was the

usual amount. Roller camshafts were tested on occasion, but were found to be less reliable than the flat tappet variety. Upon failure, bits would be sent through the engine that had a habit of getting into the oil pump and stopping it turning while the distributor continued to! Such engines were usually totally wrecked, so few left the factory with a roller camshaft fitted at this time.

One of the best engines of the early 1964-era was built by Jack Hoare. This Hi-Performance 289ci equipped with IDA Webber carburettors developed 404bhp. A very significant feature was the 12.6:1 compression, flat-top pistons, and minimum squish area between the cylinder head surface at top dead centre.

This engine was used in an open AC Cobra car by Dan Gurney and Bob Johnson at Sebring in 1964. They led the race until Bob Johnson entered the pits at night and hit a stationary Alfa Romeo with no lights on. Johnson end-for-ended the Cobra, up and over the Alfa.

The stock nodular iron Ford rocker arms, pivots, jam nuts and screw-in studs proved to be extremely reliable to 7000rpm and beyond, with very few breakages. Replacement generally occurred after 12 racing hours.

Roller rockers weren't used until 1966. Shelby American maintained a range of shorter than stock pushrods so that rocker arm corrections could be made as required. When the engines were being assembled, the correct length pushrods would be selected based on the altitude of the rocker arm in the full lift position. This was determined 'by eye' rather than with jigs or a measuring system.

The top coolant transfer passageways on the inlet manifold side of the cylinder heads were welded-over by Kelly's Block Welding Service. The

cylinder heads were then surfaced, removing 0.025in to true them. It wasn't possible to remove much more than this because the deck area wasn't all that thick to begin with. About 0.050in was the maximum Shelby American ever went to – more would result distortion problems during engine operation. The corresponding hole in the block was blanked-off using an Allen headed grub screw. This was done as an 'elimination of a possible problem' measure to prevent a coolant leak. There wasn't a major leakage problem as such for the vast majority of racing applications, except for engines prepared for long-distance events like Le Mans, which suffered head gasket problems. An effective, yet expensive solution was the development of the Cooper mechanical joint 'O'-ring with composite material 'periphery mattress' head gasket arrangement for the 1967 Le Mans. The actual mechanical joint 'O'-ring had been used successfully in conjunction with a dry-deck block and cylinder head system on the 1963 Indianapolis 500 pushrod V8 engine. The periphery mattress arrangement replaced the dry-deck element in the 1967 setup, locating the 'O'-rings and sealing the coolant that passed from the block into the cylinder heads.

Although composite head gaskets were used on the stock Hi-Performance 289ci engine, 0.025in thick Ford steel shim head gaskets were available from 1966 for racing purposes. The use of steel shim head gaskets was purely to increase the compression ratio. Once the cylinder heads were planed by 0.025in following welding, the block decks were always skimmed to be parallel to the crankshaft axis with 0.022-0.025in of clearance between the piston crown and cylinder head at top dead centre. The objective was to achieve the minimum gap necessary for optimum flame propagation purposes while ensuring that connecting rod stretch and piston rock was taken into account so that the crown of the piston didn't touch the cylinder head at maximum rpm. This resulted in more power than if the gap was the usual 0.040-0.050in.

The diameter of the inlet valves on the C3AE-6015-N Hi-Performance 289ci cylinder head was increased from 1.670in to 1.875in, and the diameter of the exhausts went from 1.450in to 1.625in. Dual contra-wound coil valve springs from Ford replaced the original Hi-Performance 289ci single coil spring fitted with a flat wound damper. Valve pressures ranged from 130–150lb seated to 350lb fully open valve lift of 0.500in. The inlet and exhaust ports were opened out as much as it was deemed possible. The combustion chamber received the same treatment, but without reducing the volume more than necessary; volume was often reduced from a nominal 49cc to 44cc by planing. The larger inlet and exhaust valves were supplied by Thompson and TRW.

Although Shelby American had the equipment to rework the cylinder heads in-house, it used outside contractors, such as Valley Head Services, Rogers Porting Service and Mondello Porting Services, to port the heads to its specifications. Then the valve seat cutting and combustion chamber machining would be completed in-house.

The AC Ace sports cars were fitted with cast iron paired 'Y'-type AC exhaust systems. Two adjacent exhaust ports were paired and the resulting two main pipes ran along the side of the car, exhausting to atmosphere just before the rear wheelarch. This manifold system meant that consecutive firing cylinders seven and eight exhausted one after the other into the same main

pipe, which wasn't desirable at all. A four-into-one-type of exhaust system per side followed. With the arrival of the Mustang, 4-2-1 or 'tri-wy' exhaust manifold systems were mostly used, as optimum mid-range torque was a major requirement for road racing. The two main pipes would exit one each side of the car, and frequently just before the rear wheelarch. The two main pipes were not linked by a 'joining pipe.' Other systems were tried, such as the 'cross-over,' but they were very complicated to install, expensive to buy, and prone to damage.

Various ignition systems were tried in 1963, such as aftermarket dual-point distributors and magnetos, but ultimately, Ford's own FoMoCo dual-point distributor was predominantly used. This was certainly the case up until 1966 when Ford's transistor ignition system was introduced. This system came after the failure of a set of points in a distributor denied a race win.

All engines were initially set with 16 degrees of cranking speed ignition timing, which equated to 36 degrees of total ignition timing. The total ignition timing of each engine was set between 36-38 degrees, depending on how the engine responded during dyno testing. If an engine required 37 degrees to develop its maximum torque and brake horse power, then that's exactly what it was set with. Total ignition timing never exceeded 38 degrees.

Shelby American fielded two Daytona Coupes (CSX2287 and CSX2299) fitted with mostly stock components and Shelby American modified Hi-Performance 289 V8 engines for the 1964 Le Mans. The event was as a great accolade to the Hi-Performance 289 engine, illustrating its performance capabilities. The aerodynamic design of the two AC

Cobra based cars meant the engines could consistently power them down the Mulsanne Straight at speeds of around 190mph. Car CSX2287 driven by Chris Amon and Jochen Neerpasch led the race in its tenth hour when the engine failed to restart after a pit stop. A loose generator drive belt had caused a flat battery. Rules stated that each car's engine must start via the starter motor fitted to it. The power source had to be the battery carried in the car, the battery could not be changed, and a supplementary battery or push-start was not permitted. The Shelby American crew inverted another battery across the terminals of the flat battery to start the engine and re-enter the race. Use of an alternative battery in such a situation was acceptable, but the team should have let the engine run for about 5 minutes to charge the battery, then switched the engine off and restarted it using the car's own battery. A french pit marshal, although technically not allowed to help, did try to indicate what was required to remain within the rules, but the crew didn't quite understand and so carried out an illegal restart. Ever vigilant Ferrari, that had someone watching the Shelby American crew's every move, spotted this and immediately protested. The protest resulted in the Cobra Coupe being disqualified more or less on the spot. If the battery incident hadn't occurred and the car had gone the distance without any other problems, the first attempt by Carroll Shelby at Le Mans with a Hi-Performance 289ci-powered AC Cobra could have had a very different result.

The second car (CSX2299) driven by Dan Gurney and Bob Bondurant was about half a lap behind when the first exited the race following the protest by Ferrari. It was going very well, slowly catching the Ferraris in front. The car had been refuelled and completed around 15 further laps when driver Dan Gurney noticed oil pressure was dropping when cornering. He drove the car into the pits to have the matter investigated, and a small stone was found to have damaged the oil cooler, causing it to steadily leak oil. The pit crew attempted to add more oil, but was told it couldn't because the car had not completed enough laps since refuelling, so the car was sent straight back out, and was driven very carefully, using minimal revs to preserve oil, before it could be brought back in to have oil and fuel added. While the car was completing the necessary number of laps a by-pass tube arrangement was prepared. This fixed the leak but made the oil cooler inoperative, so oil temperature increased to 300°F, and Dan Gurney was again forced to slow down; maximum possible oil temperature was 325°F, but this couldn't be sustained for long without wrecking the engine. These unfortunate circumstances put the lead out of reach, although car CSX2299 won its class after completing the 24-hour race about 1½ laps down on the outright winner.

The engines from both cars were stripped down after the event, and nothing was found to be wrong, despite the treatment CSX2299's engine had been subjected to throughout the race.

There was also nothing to suggest that CSX2287's engine would not also have lasted the distance given the chance. Overall, this was a remarkable feat from the basic Hi-Performance 289ci Ford V8 engine, made even more so by the fact that the drivers revved the engines to as much as 6800rpm during the race after being instructed to avoid going above 6500rpm when going through the gears or down the Mulsanne Straight.

Special parts from Ford weren't available for the Hi-Performance 289 engine as used in Shelby American-prepared AC Cobra and Mustang cars 1963-1965. Ford 'Heavy Duty' Hi-Performance 289ci C6FE coded racing parts were introduced for these engines in 1966, and then came the C7FE items of 1967: FE in this instance stood for 'Racing Part' and was applicable to the small block Fairlane V8 engine. Maximum power was increased from the 390-400bhp at 7000rpm available 1963-1965 to 430-450bhp at a maximum permissible 7500rpm for 1967.

For 1966, Ford released new cast iron, big valve, big port cylinder heads as a bolt-on kit with part number S7MR-6049-A, as well as forged pistons and stronger connecting rods.

For 1967, Ford made available a new four-bolt main cap block, a forged steel and cross-drilled crankshaft, along with improved pistons and connecting rods.

For 1966 and 1967, Ford made available its special FE small block racing parts to anyone who wanted to buy them. However, the parts were expensive, so many racers continued to use stock items.

Many Shelby American-built 289ci racing engines of these years featured GT-40 update part blocks, second version C7FE6303B marked forged crankshafts, the C6FE-6200-A connecting rods, and C6FE-6049-A cylinder heads. While these modifications were costly, they resulted in an engine with better performance and reliability compared to stock component versions. It was essential to build a small block Ford racing engine using these parts to have any hope of being competitive and reliable. Stock engine parts had a definite limitation when it came to race use. Ford made it perfectly clear that these were, for the most part, quite unsuitable for such applications, which is why it offered the racing parts.

The 1967 car model year was the last to feature the Hi-Performance 289. In 1968 Ford increased capacity to 302ci via an increase in stroke from 2.870in to 3.000in, but no high-performance version followed on. The Hi-Performance 289 cubic inch small block era therefore drew to a close.

Chapter 5

Small block GT-40 engines 1964-1969

After the 1963 Indianapolis 500 race Ford decided that its all-alloy 255ci pushrod-operated V8 engine had reached its limit and would no longer be used in that application. A more powerful dual overhead camshaft (DOHC) version with four valves per cylinder was developed for the following year. The DOHC project was intended as a cylinder head conversion based on the 1963 pushrod engine block and related internal componentry.

Ford was looking to expand its racing activity by entering into long-distance road racing events such as the Daytona, Sebring, Nürburgring and Le Mans using GT sports-type cars. The all-alloy 255ci pushrod V8 Indianapolis engine was selected for use in the Ford GTs based on its availability, compactness, light weight, power output and proven reliability. The engines were de-tuned by lowering the compression ratio,

allowing them to run successfully on the lower grade fuel available in Europe at the time, and were rated at 350bhp – a reduction of 25bhp.

A Ford GT was taken to Germany to compete in the 1964 Nürburgring 1000km sports car race. While the car went well, it suffered a suspension failure and was out of the race on the 14th lap. The engine was removed and sent back to the EEE building in Dearborn where it was stripped down and checked. All looked well, until the block was inspected. The 2nd and 4th main bearing bulkheads had cracks in, which meant that the engine suffered a major failure in the race. It was clear to Ford engineers that there was a problem with the current small block engine's long-distance endurance racing durability, but the matter wasn't investigated fully due to time constraints. The aluminium block was made with thick sections, four-bolt main caps and everything else

associated with durability, yet clearly, if the engine was to be used reliably in such racing, a major re-development programme seemed necessary. Cracks had not been found in the block after the shorter duration 1963 Indianapolis 500 race, so this was an unexpected problem highlighted by the 1000km race.

There was not enough time between discovering the problem after the Nürburgring race and the start of the 1964 Le Mans event to make alternative components, etc, so the Ford GT cars were entered into the race powered by race-prepared HP-289 small block pushrod engines.

The three 200mph capable cars entered in the 1964 Le Mans definitely had the necessary pace – one car qualified 2nd, another 4th, and in the race, one car led and another set an all-time lap record – but not the durability: there were two gearbox failures and one fuel pump failure.

Therefore, the aluminium pushrod 255ci Indianapolis engine was last used in Ford GTs in 1964 at the Nurbrgring 1000Km, and the cast iron Hi-Performance 289 became the basic power plant in 1965 cars (called GT-40 as opposed to Ford GT).

Making the 255ci Indianapolis engines suitably reliable for this application wouldn't actually have been a major undertaking for Ford. Its focus had switched to the larger 427ci engine though, so the problem wasn't investigated until mid-1967, after that years Le Mans race, when it was known that the small block engine would have to be used in 1968 because of its suitable capacity. Ford did consider the 1964 DOHC version of the 255ci Indianapolis engine, which was available in the 1965 GT-40s, but it was rejected on the basis that the engine wouldn't fit into the engine bay that well due to its 'in between the camshafts' located induction system.

Ford management followed the advice of the Engine & Foundry Division and decided to focus on using the 427ci FE NASCAR engine in 1964 instead. It was already very well developed for racing purposes, and would very likely provide Ford the outright win at Le Mans it desired in the shortest possible time. The 427ci engines all used an extended skirt block design that allowed the main caps to be cross-bolted. This made for a very solid bottom end, thus eliminating the problem thought to be present in the small block engine.

With the decision to use the 427ci FE engine made, work started on the GT-40 MKII. Ford dictum of the time was to be able to say that instead of using a purpose-built, specially-designed racing engine to power its Le Mans winning cars, Ford did so using one of its regular production line engines. To a large extent this is exactly what happened, although it was very quickly realised at Ford that building an engine suitable for winning the Indianapolis 500 and various NASCAR races was not the same as for a 24-hour endurance race like Le Mans. This race is much harder on an engine, and several changes had to be made before the 427ci was entirely suitable. GT-40 MKII cars fitted with 427ci engines were entered at Le Mans in the Prototype Class with the objective being to obtain an outright win as soon as possible, which as it happened, occurred in 1966.

The basic all cast iron High Performance 289ci small block Ford engine was used in GT-40s in 1965, 1966 and 1967 at Le Mans, the best engines having up to 385bhp. Having been prepared for endurance racing, these engines were not as highly modified as other versions, although they did feature the very best special parts available from Ford at the time. For 1965 the basic HP-289ci engine was used at Le Mans almost in its entirety, which meant the pistons, rings, connecting rods, crankshaft, crankshaft damper, cylinder heads, rocker arms, head gaskets, etc. During this time these engines were used with some success in the GT-40s, but not without reliability problems such as a head gasket failure in the 1965 Le Mans. The six 325ci versions of the small block engine prepared by Shelby American performed extremely well in the same race. The two cars powered by these engines were only 6-7mph slower down the Mulsanne Straight than the 427ci engined GT-40s. This was a commendable feat indeed, although none of the Ford GT-40s finished the race that year; all broke down for various reasons. However disappointing, the reliability issues with the 289ci were of secondary importance to Ford, as management expected the big block 427ci FE engine to power its winning car.

For 1966 Ford released a strengthened version (C6FE-6015-A) of the stock production block with its two-bolt nodular iron C6FE-A main caps. The general wall thickness of the block was increased, and there were strategic localised increases, too. Note that the 'F' of the 'FE' part of the code means 'non-production racing part.' The 'E' simply means 'engine,' the same as all other Ford engine codes, and applies to small block engines. Also released for 1966 were forged raised-top pistons and improved stock-type connecting rods made from a stronger material and machined slightly differently where the connecting rod bolt heads fit to take a high strength ⅜in 'football head' bolt. This machining method and bolt head configuration left a maximum amount of material in this vital area of the connecting rod. The use of the original Hi-Performance 289ci crankshaft, supplementary counterweight and crankshaft damper was retained.

New, larger inlet and exhaust port and valve cast iron cylinder heads were available, first used in 1966 and then in 1967 at Le Mans. The inlet valves had a head diameter of 1.875in, with a 30 degree seat angle. The exhaust valves had a diameter of 1.625in, with the usual 45 degree valve seat angle. These racing cylinder heads had casting code C6FE-6090-A stamped on the left-hand end of the cylinder head, and C6FE adjacent to the two centre pushrod slots under the rocker cover area without a day/year/month casting code present. A distinguishing feature of these cylinder heads was the fact that the pushrod slots/pushrod holes were ¹⁄₁₆in further apart compared to standard, allowing for a slightly wider inlet port. They were later made available by Ford as a kit (S7MR-6049-A) or as individual cylinder heads (C6FE-6049-A), and there were also right- (C6FE-6051-B) and left-hand (C6FE-6083-B) fitting 0.032in thick companion steel shim head gaskets – the head gaskets failed in the race. The rocker arms used 1965-1967 were standard items, but selected on the basis of hardness and meeting precisely the 1.6:1 rocker ratio specification.

LE MANS 1967

Ford took 13 all cast iron 289ci small block Ford V8 engines to Le Mans in 1967. Every single engine failed in practise and in the race, all doing so around the 16-18 hour point. While the short assembly was unbelievably strong, the main bearing bulkheads of the blocks all broke in roughly the same place, the same way, and more or less, on the same part of the circuit. Each failed at the end of the Mulsanne Straight after operating at maximum rpm in top gear for about 40 seconds; the cars pushing 210-220mph. All of the broken engines were taken back to the USA and stripped down in the EEE building and the damage surveyed.

Ford engineers had used the new 'Heavy Duty' 289ci engine block (XE-136136), which was an improvement over the previous year's block. It now had four-bolt main caps on the centre three bearings as well as more material in strategic places, making it inherently stronger than the 1966 item. Note that the 'XE' part of the code stood for 'experimental non-production part.' New light weight forged pistons were used in conjunction with the heavy but unbelievable strong 1964-1965 DOHC Indianapolis 500 V8 engine connecting rods. The connecting rods were made

out of aircraft quality steel by an outside forging contractor in Detroit. They had 9/32in Pratt & Whitney aircraft bolts and a centre-to-centre distance of 5.316in, resulting in a 1.85:1 connecting rod to stroke ratio. The forged steel crankshaft was as used in the 1963-1965 Indianapolis 500 engines and matched to the Hi-Performance 289 crankshaft damper. A supplementary counterweight was not required due to there being sufficient material on the crankshaft's counterweighting. The head gasket system involved the use of Cooper mechanical joint 'O'-rings similar to those used on the 255ci Indianapolis engines, but to suit a 4in bore and a 'perifiery mattress' arrangement. This arrangement worked well, showing no signs of failure at the point that the blocks failed.

The catastrophic engine failures of 1967 were a serious problem for Ford because for 1968 there was going to be a capacity limit of 5-litres, and this was the only suitable engine it had available. So if the GT-40 was to have any chance of winning with the small block engine that year, the problem – whatever it was – would have to be well and truly solved.

Ford Engine Engineering engineer Hank Lenox was tasked with finding out what went wrong and coming up with a solution. His verdict was that the block wasn't at fault, but the crankshaft was; "A crankshaft for a V8 engine can be designed in one of two ways, for 'maximum bob-weight' or for 'minimum bearing loading.' The crankshaft design Ford had been using on these engines were of the 'maximum bob-weight'-type, which was imposing the high bearing loads on the 2nd and 4th main bearings bulkheads of the block." Lenox consequently redesigned the crankshaft after the 1967 Le Mans race, moving away from the maximum

bob-weight-type to one with minimum bearing loading, and the blocks were again made slightly stronger, in the 2nd, 3rd and 4th main bearing bulkheads. Both up-graded items were released by Ford in mid-1967 for use in all 289ci racing engine applications.

The upgraded forged crankshafts produced in mid-1967 for the GT-40 289ci engine were quite easy to recognise compared to earlier small block Ford V8 items. The third counterweight in from each end was displaced 90 degrees to the first and second counterweights, and both were displaced 180 degrees radially from each other. The crankshafts were marked C7FE6303B, and used in conjunction with the Hi-Performance 289 crankshaft damper. Early 1967 forged steel HP-289 crankshafts had the counterweighting displaced similarly to the 1963-1965 Indianapolis engines. The later 1967 counterweight configuration forged steel HP-289 crankshaft was carried over to the 1968 'Tunnel Port,' 1968 and 1969 GT-40, and 1969-1970 Boss 302ci engines in increased 3in stroke form.

LE MANS 1968-1969

Ford in the USA built and supplied about 12 sets of 302ci bottom ends in part form in both 1968 and 1969. Each set included brand new four-bolt main cap blocks, forged steel 3in stroke crankshafts, 1964-1965-type DOHC Indianapolis 500 connecting rods (1.77:1 connecting rod to stroke ratio), forged pistons, Cooper mechanical joint 'O'-ring and periphery mattress head gasket sets, plus related componentry by JW Automotive in the UK. JW Automotive built all of the small block engines for the Gulf Oil GT-40s, and both years fitted Weslake aluminium cylinder heads in conjunction with the Cooper mechanical joint 'O'-rings and periphery-type head gaskets as used by Ford in 1967.

Gurney/Weslake cylinder heads were used in 1968 and 1969, which produced about 20-25bhp more than any others tested. The cylinder head design differed slightly between each year, but both used identical 1967 William Mills/WM castings.

The basic 302ci engine was used in the winning GT-40 car (no.1075) in 1968 and 1969, both times set up to almost identical specification. These engines, with exceedingly strong but quite heavy Indianapolis connecting rods, were 100% reliable in this application. Both developed about 420-425bhp, and were absolutely safe to 7500rpm in this long-distance specification guise. With the 1969 race completed and won, the GT-40 era was over. A smaller engine capacity of three litres was introduced for 1970, and Ford withdrew the cars from competition, regarding them as obsolete.

Chapter 6

Indianapolis 500 255ci DOHC engines 1964-1965

Despite only just losing the 1963 Indianapolis 500 race, Ford engineers knew that a slightly different approach would be needed to decisively beat the Offenhauser engine; an approach more in line with what engineers of Advanced Engines suggested when management first gave the 'go ahead' to build an engine for this event. The original thinking was to build a four overhead camshaft, four valves per cylinder V8 in mid-1962, and is why the engine engineering codes are out of sequence. The 1963 pushrod engine, which was the first engine used at Indianapolis, had engine code AX230, while the later 1964 double overhead camshaft (DOHC) engine had engine code AX227. The DOHC engine had already been assigned a code number when engineers were instructed to go with a pushrod engine instead. When it was decided to produce a DOHC type of engine the original code (AX227) was simply reactivated.

At the beginning of June 1963 a group was formed to design and develop the DOHC version of the stock production 260ci small block Ford V8 engine under code AX227. The engineers involved were: Ed Pinkerton – Principal Engineer; Dick Tabin – Engine Powertrain (crankshaft, connecting rods, rings and bearings); Bill Gelgota – major castings (blocks and cylinder heads); Gerry Schley – valve train & lubrication (camshafts, seals, valves, valve springs, valve spring retainers, gears, and oil pumps); John Carlini – dyno-testing coordinator, with Bill Phillips and Charley Teezar both doing the dyno tests; Bill Barr – intake and exhaust systems, cam covers, fuel injection, engine ventilation. The inlet and exhaust porting criteria was completed by Rick Krygwoski. Those that undertook the analytical, procurement, machine shop, expeditor work previously were also all involved in the new engine project.

Unlike the 1963 pushrod engine, the DOHC engine was fraught with design failures throughout most components, and engineers went through test engines at an unexpected rate; about ten complete engines were lost (damaged beyond further use). The initial plan was to build just two Series I engines or modified 1963 engines fitted with DOHC, four valve per cylinder heads and exhaust pipes in the same position as on the pushrod engines; and two Series II engines with similar design cylinder heads, but the exhaust pipes situated in the valley of the engine, and above the engine were the carburettors, as on the 1963 engine. After a decision about what design configuration was best, about 10-12 Series III (final design) engines were planned, and these would then be used for racing purposes.

The development issues faced were near unbelievable, as every minor and major part had to be redesigned to achieve reliability, and the breakage problems experienced were not foreseen. The problems arose from the need to achieve higher revs from the DOHC engine, and there wasn't a single part that didn't need to be revised. The 1963 pushrod engine operated at around 7200-7400rpm and higher, but the DOHC was required to turn at 8600-8800rpm and above – ultimately, it turned to 9700rpm.

Some of the changes were simple revisions, such as the crankshaft that went from SAE 3550 material to SAE 4340, and finally to electric furnace grade SAE 4340. The original 1963 Indy connecting rods stretched almost 0.060in under test conditions every time the piston went through an exhaust stroke at 9200rpm. This meant that the piston crowns were making contact with the squish areas of the cylinder heads, causing sealing ring gaskets to fail, so the 'squish height' had to be changed. Ultimately, this involved a complete 'clean sheet of paper' redesign of the connecting rods. The new connecting rods were very strong and featured a centre-to-centre distance of 5.316in, which in conjunction with the 2.870in stroke, gave the engine a 1.85:1 connecting rod to stroke ratio.

The gudgeon pin end clearance had to be reduced to a maximum of 0.005in to prevent the gudgeon pins pushing the circlips out the side of the piston. The piston design generally had to be revised, as the original was not robust enough. Experiments with two ring pistons (one compression ring, one oil scraper) didn't prove satisfactory, and considering the time constraints, had to be abandoned.

Other problems encountered with the cylinder block included: front engine cover; valve springs; the mains pressure oil pump; the two scavenge pumps; the distributor and fuel pump drives; oil flow volume to the camshaft lobes and camshaft followers interfaces; and intake manifold shape and sizes.

There was excessive crankcase pressure and poor ventilation so the engine was sealed from atmospheric pressure. The oil scavenge pump sizes were increased, and all of the air from the crankcase, camshaft gear drive train and camshaft areas was removed by over-scavenging, so that the engine ran with 10-15in of vacuum.

The original cylinder head configuration with three sparkplugs per cylinder was no longer satisfactory; there wasn't enough coolant in the cylinder head or enough coolant flow, so a redesign was necessary. The flow of water through the cylinder head was found to be inadequate, and coolant was becoming trapped in certain areas of the head and boiling, especially around the sparkplugs. This three sparkplug cylinder head setup was well investigated. A single Ford-made distributor was used to fire all of the sparkplugs, and it was a 'three stack' arrangement with 24 high tension wires coming out of it. The three sections of the distributor were able to be switched on or off while the engine was running, to see what happened with all of the various sparkplug firing combinations in operation. There were problems with induction firing of cylinders because of the lengths of the wires and their close proximity to each other on the installation.

The fuel injection pump and distributor were originally located to the rear of the camshafts, so that the front of the engine remained uncluttered, and also to make these items easily accessible for servicing. However, this arrangement no longer worked because the non-constant angular rotational velocity of the camshafts ruined the componentry in no time. As a result, the fuel injection pump and distributor were moved to the front of the engine, but this also caused problems, although none as severe. The solution was to use short spline-ended shafts to take the drive forward to the fuel pump and the distributor, and a small alternator located low down on the right-hand side of the engine was gear driven off the camshaft gear train.

A starter motor wasn't fitted to these engines. They were started by engaging a coupling at the back of the gearbox. The coupling was connected to the main-shaft of the gearbox. With the clutch engaged and the gearbox in neutral, drive went straight through to the engine. A handheld starter motor with a triple battery pack was used to turn the engine over, the driver throwing the ignition switch when the engine was being motored over. With the electric GE engine dynamometer, the engine was of course started by motoring the engine to 500rpm by the dynamometer and then switching on the ignition, at which point the engine would fire and start. That's the advantage of these types of engine dynamometer. Not only is the armature an electric motor that can turn or motor the engine over, once started it becomes a generator with the engine driving it.

Overall the engine project was an enormous task, due to so much unexpectedly going wrong, but everything was solved in time for the 1964 Indianapolis 500 race.

EXTRACTS FROM SAE PAPER S397 – THE FORD DOHC COMPETITION ENGINE

By A J Scussel – Ford Motor Company Metropolitan Section New York, New York, May 7th, 1964.

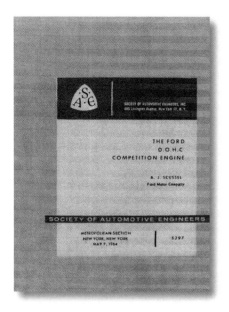

Introduction

The success of last year's combination of our light weight pushrod engine and the Lotus car was a strong factor in the decision to make major revisions for the 1964 race engine. It seems reasonably certain that a number of race car designers would incorporate some of the features of the Lotus-Ford combination in their 1964 entries. This would result in significantly higher performance in this year's race. Since the 1963 pushrod engine had delivered close to its ultimate capability in achieving 375bhp from its 255ci/4.2-litre displacement and weighing 360lb/164kg, it seemed necessary to change the design to be competitive.

Objectives for the 1964 engine

As a result of analysis of competitive experiences in 1963 the following objectives were established for the 1964 engine:

1 – Make the Indianapolis 1964 versions of the Fairlane engine as competitive

horsepower-wise as possible at the minimum feasible rpm.
2 – Hold the total engine weight to 400lb/182kg.
3 – Utilise gasoline/petrol to maintain a stock car image.
4 – Retain carburettors if possible, or adopt some known fuel injection system.

These four objectives pose some very formidable tasks. The first objective implied an increase in horsepower in the order of 50, or about 13%. The 1963 figure would have to be raised to approximately 420-425bhp within the 255ci displacement limitation of the Indianapolis race. The second objective was equally difficult, as it required the increased performance to be obtained with only an 11% increase in engine weight over the 1963 figure of 360lb/164kg. Finally, the third and forth objectives had to be achieved within the known performance standard of the opposition. A better appreciation of the problem is provided by the engine power comparisons of torque and

horsepower shown in Figure 1. The datum is, of course, the performance curves of the 1963 Offenhauser engine and Ford V8 race engine.

Development plan

Once the programme objectives had been established it was imperative to undertake a critical analysis of their design implications and then formulate a plan of action for the design, development and fabrication of both experimental and race engines. Among the first criteria yielded by our analyses was the establishment of 8000rpm as the approximate level necessary for achieving our horsepower objective. The valve gear and induction system limitation of the pushrod engine indicated the need for a DOHC configuration. Once determination had been made to pursue this configuration it was necessary to defer consideration of the other objectives until we designed, built and tested our first experimental overhead camshaft engines. At this point a three phase development plan for the total programme was laid out.

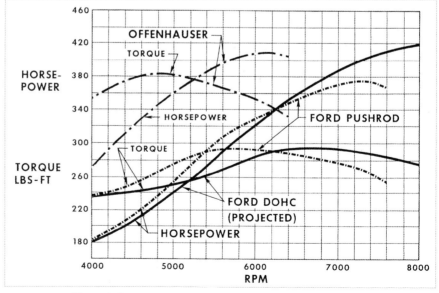

Figure 1. Power comparison: 1964 projected vs 1963 actual.

Phase 1 would involve the design, fabrication and evaluation of a double overhead cam engine that would utilise as many as possible of the basic components of the 1963 pushrod engine. Phase 2 would provide for a new series of experimental engines incorporating design changes resulting from the analysis of Phase 1 test results, with special attention to combustion chamber configuration, induction system design and multiple ignition points in the combustion chamber (twin sparkplugs). Phase 3 would essentially be the Indianapolis 500 race engine, incorporating all design changes validated by tests and evaluations resulting from Phase 1 and 2. Testing during Phase 3 would result in incorporation of design refinements in the final engines right up to race day.

The programme began building an engine using the cylinder block, crankshaft, connecting rods, bearings, water pump, oil pumps, alternator, oil pan and component gear drives of the 1963 engine. The purpose of this first experimental engine was to provide the factual basis for the following:

1 – Determination of which 1963 basic components could be retained.
2 – Corroboration of the analytical studies on horsepower objectives.
3 – A test of the design of the overhead camshaft components.
4 – Evaluation of the fuel system.
5 – Evaluation of the engine – racing car chassis integration.

Both dynamometer and racing car testing of the Phase 1 engine confirmed that the cylinder block and reciprocating and rotating components carried over from the 1963 engine were more than adequate to withstand the highest demands in engine speeds and loads which would be made by

the 1964 competition. These tests also indicated that a four-valve, pent-roof combustion chamber design would permit a peak of more than 400bhp to be achieved at approximately 8000rpm. The particular combustion chamber of this first design exhibited a deficiency. Dynamometer tests in Dearborn and actual racing car tests at the Indianapolis Speedway confirmed that an engine with a chamber of this design when using gasoline/petrol, would not permit sufficient cooling around the valves. A redesigned combustion chamber was incorporated in engines built after this.

Although our objectives called for carburettors, we anticipated some difficulty in obtaining the right size ones. Accordingly, our early testing of fuel injection prevented any development delay when the non-availability of suitable sized carburettors was confirmed. These tests demonstrated rather conclusively that the basic Hilborn constant flow fuel system modified for use with gasoline/petrol would be our choice. In an actual

track comparison between carburettor and fuel injection at Indianaoplis one of our Phase 1 engines was tested in a racing car with the 58mm Weber carburettors used on 1963 pushrod engines, and then with a Hilborn fuel injection system. Both systems worked equally well, with the Hilborn system slightly superior in terms of fuel economy. However, this latter fact was attributable to a characteristic of the Weber carburettor installation by which we were, to a small extent, unwittingly penalized [the air/fuel mixture was being sucked up and out of the tops of the carburettors when at full throttle] last year (1963). The Weber carburettors had been designed to have minimum ram length between the air entrance to the air horns and the valve. The length we used produced pulse reversals which back-flowed fuel through the carburettor to the air stream. Several gallons of fuel were probably lost in the 1963 race because of this.

Installation of the Phase 1 engine in the test car revealed problems in routing the exhaust pipes around chassis

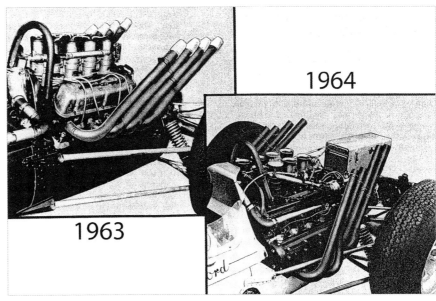

Figure 2. Exhaust wrap-around.

components. With the conventional exhaust port placement on an overhead cam V8 engine the primary exhaust pipes leave the engine at a very low position, so some of the these pipes had to be routed through the rear suspension linkage arms. This awkward and complicated routing led us to interchange positions of the intake and exhaust systems (see Figure 2). The rear engine location made this possible.

Phase 2 engines were built primarily to refine the fuel injection system and study whether more than one sparkplug source would improve combustion. Several cylinder heads were built to permit installation of up to three sparkplugs per chamber. Distributor arrangements providing selective firing either singularly or in combination gave a very thorough evaluation of combustion characteristics as a function of ignition sources and timing.

Our Phase 3 engine, for all practical purposes, is the Indianapolis race engine; however, design refinements may be incorporated almost to race day. For the Phase 3 engine we have designed six exhaust systems to meet the requirements

of car builders. Tests at Kingman in Arizona show that the valley location of the exhaust system is superior because of less aerodynamic drag and better tuning – to include 180 degree pulse tuning. The foregoing has provided a brief description of the three phases of our development programme and the identification of the principal design problems associated with each.

Test and analytical data

Track testing. Up to the time of this writing there have been five periods of track testing, and very briefly, the purpose and results of these track testing were as follows:

A – Indianapolis, October 1963

To evaluate the Phase 1 engine in a racing car, and to assess in a preliminary way the use of fuel injection in place of carburettors. The results confirmed the basic soundness of the DOHC engine for intensive development, and the acceptability of the Hilborn constant flow fuel injection system. The results also confirmed several anticipated deficiencies of the

initial design, and disclosed certain other deficiencies that only testing could uncover. Among these were oil leaks and 'oil pullover' via the breather.

B – Kingman, Arizona, January & February 1964

The purpose of this period of track testing was to provide confirmation of changes made after the Indianapolis tests, all of which had received preliminary validation in dynamometer testing at Dearborn. This track testing period also provided the initial shakedown for the Phase 3 engine (with the exhaust in the valley of the Vee and the inlets in between the camshafts) and the first comparisons of the new valley exhaust configurations. The results of the January testing period focused attention on the need for a new attack on the 'oil pullover' problem (throwing oil out of the breather system) to ensure that it didn't happen at high revs. A solution was found and its effectiveness was confirmed in the February period of testing at Kingman in 1964. The solution was to run the engine with negative crankcase pressure (crankcase was under vacuum HG).

C – Indianapolis, March 1964

This period of testing provided the first opportunity to assess the overall performance of our Phase 3 engine design at the Speedway. It also made possible the testing of several engines in the specific racing car for which they were intended to be used in. Some of the typical refinements which this testing period produced were those associated with the calibration of the fuel injection system.

Dynamometer testing

Dynamometer testing activities were extensive and occurred in each of

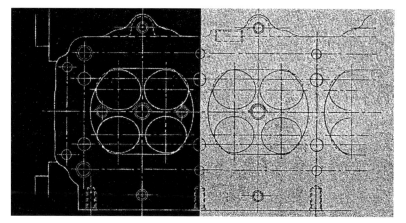

Figure 3. Cylinder head. The left-hand drawing of the combustion chamber shows three sparkplugs on the centre line. The drawing on the right shows a single, centrally-positioned sparkplug on the same centre line.

Figure 4. Phase 2 engine on the Ford dynamometer at Dearborn.

It's well known that with methanol the fuel/air ratio must be rich compared to gasoline/petrol because of its low heating value. The high heat of vaporisation results in internal cooling of the engine. Some engine temperatures recorded at Phoenix proved very interesting. With a given installation, we recorded 214°F/100°C water and 225°F/108°C oil at an ambient temperature of 95°F/35°C using gasoline/petrol. Under the same conditions when using methanol the water temperature was 176°F/80°C and the oil temperature 185°F/85°C.

Crankshaft vibration damping

It was also necessary to confirm that our crankshaft vibration damper could control crankshaft torsional deflections at speeds of up to 8000rpm. It did, as can be seen from the damped and un-damped torsional deflection curves in Figure 6. Our calculated natural

the three separate phases of the development programme. As a matter of fact, dynamometer testing of the Phase 2 engines was sufficiently conclusive to not require in-car testing of those engines.

Performance testing of the Phase 2 engines was focused on obtaining our objective of 420bhp at 8000rpm. Once this had been accomplished, we concentrated on developing the best possible torque curve by varying the camshaft timing and overlap with several intake manifolds and valve sizes. The desired results was attained with peak horsepower of 425bhp at 8000rpm and peak torque of 295lb-ft at 6400rpm. The maximum brake mean effective pressure (bmep) was 175psi.

Gasoline/petrol versus methanol

At this point, it was decided to determine the increase in engine performance with methanol as a fuel. The only change made on the engine at this time was to revise the fuel system

to handle the increased fuel flow. The results have been superimposed on the gasoline/petrol power figures for comparison purposes (Figure 5).

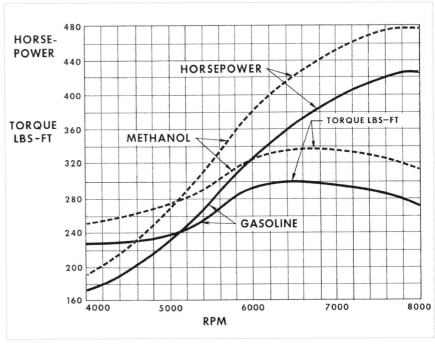

Figure 5. 1964 Horsepower and torque gasoline-methanol comparison.

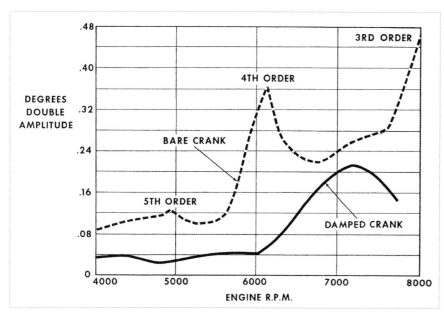

Figure 6. Crankshaft torsion vs rpm. The dotted line represents the degrees of double amplitude (DDA) when the engine was run up on the dynamometer without a crankshaft damper fitted. The solid line represents the DDA with the Schwitzer designed elastomer type damper fitted. The highest recorded .21 DDA is within Ford's normal requirement (.25 DDA) to ensure crankshaft reliability (won't break a crankshaft in service).

through design changes, which will be discussed in connection with the respective development features.

Analytical data

The analytical data which we required in carrying out the programme were of two kinds; that's those deriving from our 1963 experience, and those which we found necessary to acquire during the evolution of the 1964 development. In the former group were those that provided a point of departure for our initial decisions, that is, the Indianapolis track survey information, track acceleration and deceleration characteristics, and air flow comparisons. In the second group was such information as stoichiometric ratios (that's air/fuel ratios), exhaust configuration tuning and aerodynamic drag, and heat generation and distribution.

The latter one among these is interesting to examine at this point. This set of data (Figure 7) derives from the total engine heat and its distribution as a function of engine speed. This

frequency of 24,600 CPM (Cycles Per Minute) was also confirmed.

In addition to yielding data pertinent to the design characteristics, our dynamometer testing served the other vital purpose of evaluating the durability of the design. In view of the time urgency in our schedule, durability testing had to proceed in parallel with the development testing. A speed and load dynamometer cycle was established on the basis of the Indianapolis track data we had. It consisted of five hours at full load with 30 seconds cycling in engine speed between 6300rpm and 8100rpm in the following sequence and approximate duration: 6300-7200rpm in 6 seconds; 7200-6300rpm in 3 seconds: 6300-8100rpm in 15 seconds; 8100-6300rpm

Figure 7. Total engine heat and distribution.

in 6 seconds. 600 such cycles at full load revealed several sources of possible failure. All were corrected

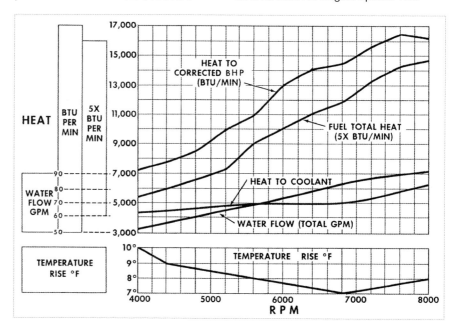

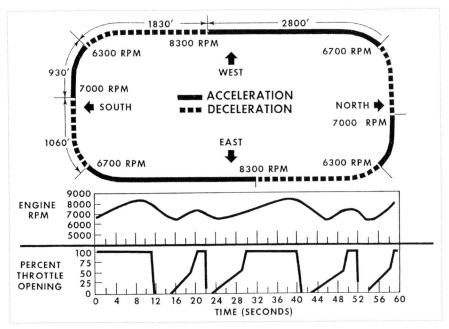

Figure 8. Ford test vehicle, Indianapolis track, 25th March 1964: average speed 153.8mph.

includes heat to the coolant, as well as water flow and temperature rise. It will be noted that the heat generated is in the order of 73,00 BTU/min (British Thermal Units) at 8000rpm. Brake horse power (bhp) accounts for 16,000-17,000 BTU and about 6200 BTU is delivered to the coolant. The water flow at 8000rpm is approximately 92 gallons per minute. There is an actual temperature fall of 2°F between engine operation at 4000rpm versus 8000rpm.

At this point, I should like to return to two items of data upon which we based important technical decisions at the outset of this engine development programme. The first of these is the track acceleration and deceleration characteristics. We carefully analysed the considerable amount of information obtained from our 1963 race entries. Using these as a datum in conjunction with the projected increase in engine performance to be achieved by our 1964 engine, we were able to work out the required acceleration and

deceleration pattern to lap faster than before.

Figure 8 shows the engine characteristics, in one racing car during the March 1964 Indianapolis test, such as engine speed and throttle opening for a typical lap of the Indianapolis Speedway. The best average lap speed during this test period was 153.8mph (246km/h). To accomplish this, the driver reached a peak speed of 183mph (294km/h) down the straight section of the track, and completed the 2.5m (4km) lap in just over 58.5 seconds. During this particular lap the engine speed

varied between 6700rpm and 8300rpm on the straight sections, decreased to 6300rpm entering the turns, and reached 7000rpm on the short, straight sections between the turns. Although this was the performance of a single racing car and driver on a single lap, we felt that it was sufficiently typical of the desired pattern to warrant using this data for our dynamometer durability cycling regime.

The second example of analytical information which was carefully assessed at the beginning of Phase 1 is that concerning the air flow characteristics required for the new engine design. A Lotus racing car with the Phase 1 engine was placed in a wind tunnel and on a rolling road dynamometer, so that track conditions could be simulated as closely as possible while being in a laboratory environment.

Calculations were made of valve lift, and piston velocity as a function of crankshaft angle, on the basis of the higher engine speeds for a number of valve and port configurations. Examination of this data showed that in the four-valve configuration the vertical port would provide adequate airflow

Figure 9. Wind tunnel testing.

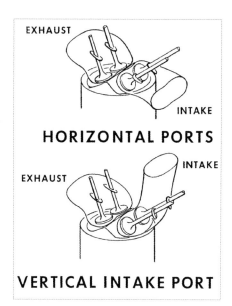

HORIZONTAL PORTS

VERTICAL INTAKE PORT

Figure 10.

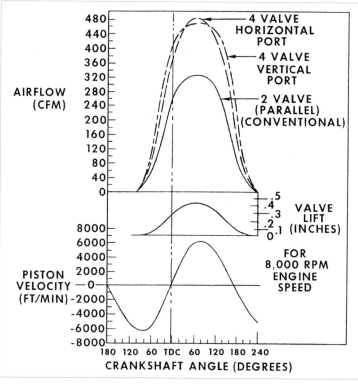

Figure 11.

characteristics for our purposes (see Figure 10).

The next step was to calculate the inlet port, valve throat and valve head sizes. A maximum inlet velocity of 270 feet per second at 8000rpm was established as the flow criteria at the smallest cross-sectional area in the valve throat. From this, the total intake throat area could be readily calculated, and the internal diameter of the valve insert could be determined taking into account the reduction of the throat area by the valve stem. This, of course, would fix the valve seat and valve head diameter sizes. The port area was 2.82in^2 at the valves and increased gradually to 4.02in^2 at the throttle body mounting face.

It was next assumed that the valve curtain area should be 10% greater than the throat area. From this, the valve lift was established. These calculations fixed the valve head diameter for the inlets at 37.0mm (1.460in), and 34.5mm (1.360in) for the exhausts, with a lift of 11.1mm (0.440in). Fixing these parameters made

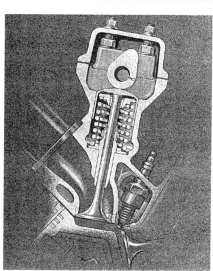

Figure 12. Port and valve detail.

it possible to design a combustion chamber and piston dome to produce the required 12.5:1 compression ratio. Some of these design details are shown in Figure 12.

During the early dynamometer testing period we sought confirmation of our initial determinations. Several variants with respect to valve sizes, valve lifts, and camshaft timings were used to bracket combinations. For example, inlet and exhaust valve head diameter sizes of between 34.5-39.7mm (1.360-1.560in) were tried. The final combination settled on was 37.0mm (1.460in) for the inlets and 34.5mm (1.360in) for the exhausts, and valve lift of 11.1mm (0.440in) for both valves.

Details of development

General – In the description of our 1964 engine that deals with the details of the engine development, it's useful to refer to a transverse view (Figure 12) and a longitudinal view of the engine (Figure 13).

A logical point of departure for examining the details of the engine

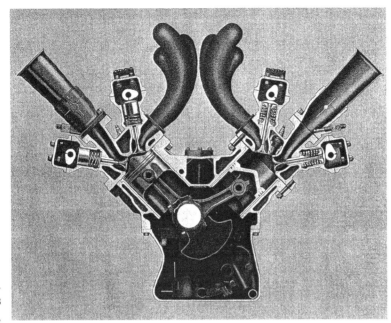

Figure 13.
Phase 3
engine.

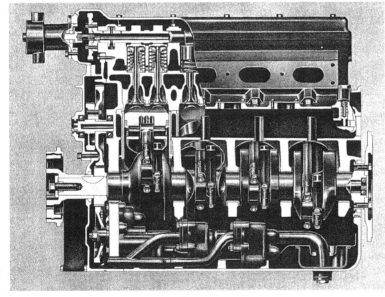

Figure 14.
Phase 3
engine.

B – Crankshaft (with additional counterweighting).
C – Ignition system (mechanical changes in distributor and mounting).
D – Alternator.
E – Water pump.
F – Oil pan (with new baffling).

All of these had proven themselves in 1963, and our analysis had shown that they had the capability of functioning reliably in the higher speed range of our 1964 engine.

In view of the excellent performance of the Ford 'breakerless' ignition system in 1963, it was naturally considered, along with other possible systems. It was adopted for the 1964 engine when we found that it performed satisfactorily at the higher engine speeds required. Certain design refinements were necessary, primarily in the mechanical elements of the distributor and its external configuration. A block diagram and photograph (see Figure 14) of the Ford transistorized breakerless ignition system, as modified for the 1964 engine, show both the functional relationship and the external changes that have been made.

The Ford ignition system employs a variable reluctance for achieving voltage control in the triggering of the main ignition circuit. The design employs a concentric permanent magnet and coil, with a toothed rotor which varies the reluctance (resistance) of the magnetic circuit as it rotates, thus permitting the achievement of the proper waveform to trigger the main ignition circuit. Because the latter circuit is fully transistorized the design attains compactness and high reliability. The circuit permits a spark coil to deliver an almost constant voltage throughout the entire high speed range.

The operation characteristics of the 1964 engine made it possible to eliminate a spark advance mechanism.

development is provided by a brief description of those elements of the 1963 engine which were retained. It will be remembered that for the Phase 1 engine certain features which were originally retained were later discarded, for example the Weber carburettors. Accordingly, reference is now made only to those elements actually incorporated in the final design.

Retained elements

The engine elements retained from 1963 are:

A – Cylinder block and main bearings.

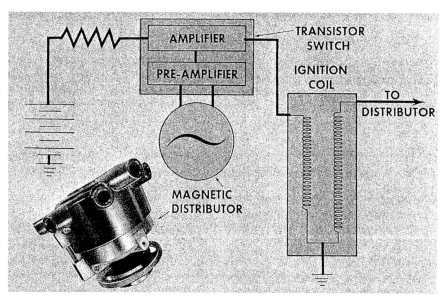

Figure 15. Ford breakerless transistor ignition system.

The dynamometer determinations of spark requirements established a fixed amount of total ignition timing of 52 degrees before top dead centre (BTDC). A retard device was incorporated for starting purposes. Vehicle testing established a cranking speed of 500rpm.

Whereas the engine idles between 2000 and 2500rpm, idling speed could not be fixed at a specific figure because each driver seems to have a particular preference or 'feel' of engine response when operating from closed to open throttle in the turns.

Three heat ranges of the Autolite racing sparkplugs were found to be necessary to meet the varying conditions of weather and vehicle calibration.

New elements
The new elements of the design are:

A – Valve gear (including camshafts and associated gear trains and housings).
B – Cylinder heads with 'pent-roof' combustion chambers (induction and valving).
C – Connecting rods (stronger ones).
D – Fuel injection system.
E – Lubrication system (sump pumps and scavenging).
F – Exhaust system.

For the first Phase 1 engine (see Figure 16) operational experience

Figure 16. Phase 1 engine fitted with Weber carburettors in the centre of the vee, and exhaust ports on the lower side of the cylinder head.

was needed as quickly as possible; consequently, recognised design deficiencies were accepted. For example, there was a definite weakness in this design in that the distributor drive and fuel injection drive are mounted at the rear of the camshaft. The torsional wind-up of the camshaft made a spark scatter that was beyond anything we could hope to use. Our Phase 1 development testing at Indianapolis made this stand out very clearly. We redesigned the engine to mount these components on the front cover. However, we were then faced with the task of designing an extremely compact distributor to clear racing car components. This caused a drive coupling problem during our durability testing, which was finally solved with an intermediate driveshaft splined at each end to fit into the front of the top two camshafts, and into the fuel pump and distributor.

Camshafts
A camshaft lobe and follower are shown in Figure 12 (upper aspect of the diagram). The cam lobe is designed for working against a cup-type follower with a cylindrical surface. These are steel camshafts which ride against a steel tappet that has been chrome plated for wear resistance. There is a bearing for the camshaft in each instance between adjacent cylinders. This type of tappet requires a key, which is visible on the right-hand side of each tappet. It fits in a groove in the cylinder

head and prevents the tappet rotating. We tried early in the program to run this camshaft without oil holes at each individual cam lobe. This proved to be unacceptable in that we picked up metal particles and had galling-type failures early in our test cycle. We have since drilled small holes in the base circle of each camshaft lobe, and the camshafts are all drilled throughout their length to carry oil to each lobe in view of the critical camshaft lobe-tappet relationship.

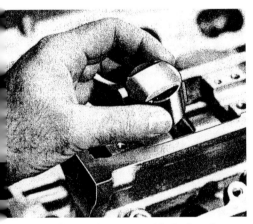

Figure 17. Tappet with the location key just visible on the right-hand side, and the cylindrical surface that the camshaft lobe wipes over in the middle of the top of the tappet.

It might be well at this point to digress briefly to consider the development of the camshaft with relation to both timing and phasing. The previously mentioned analytical study of the induction system established a valve lift of 11.1mm (0.044in) as being the most desirable from the standpoint of combustion chamber geometry. Several camshaft contours were designed, with the durations all occurring within 300-348 degree span. Design studies indicated that the effective valve event should be limited to approximately 300 degrees of duration. With these

events, a minimum piston to valve clearance of 1.0mm (0.040in) was maintained. Also, it was possible to obtain a compression ratio of 12.5:1 and still provide for a reasonable valve overlap. Bench tests using a test rig were conducted at an engine speed of 9000rpm, with various camshaft lobes having acceleration lying between 0.0177-0.0355mm (0.0007-0.0014in) of lift per 0.2 degrees of camshaft rotation. Oscilloscopic analysis was made of several valve springs and camshaft lobes to determine their most suitable characteristics. A study of the curves indicated a 360lb total valve spring load and a camshaft lobe design that did not exceed 0.0177mm (0.0007in) of lift per 0.2 degree of camshaft rotation acceleration were satisfactory. A set of dual valve springs were then designed with an open load of 360lb and a closed load of 95lb. The two contra-wound valve springs have an effective interference fit of 0.4mm (0.015in) for damping purposes, and the two springs natural frequencies differ by 5000 cycles per minute (cpm). The outer valve spring is 28,000cpm and the inner 33,000cpm.

Subsequent dynamometer testing established that the best overall horsepower and torque characteristics were obtained with a 306 degree duration camshaft phase, so that there was 87 degrees of valve overlap at top dead centre (TDC). The required valve lash was 0.375mm (0.015in) for the inlet valves and 0.45mm (0.018in) for the exhaust valves on a cold engine. There is no mechanical valve lash adjustment on the current design. Adjustments are made by either grinding the end of

the valve stem to increase the tappet clearance or selecting tappets with the correct head thickness.

Camshaft drive

The selection of the method of driving the camshafts in an overhead camshaft engine is a most controversial subject. For our engine, the selection was not very difficult. When you consider that we required a very reliable high speed drive where cost and noise were not a prime factor, straight cut spur gears were the obvious answer. The pushrod engine last year had already established its reliability since it had employed steel spur gears for the camshaft, water pump, oil pump and alternator. It was decided to use this type of drive system as the basic portion of the gear train, and merely add the required gears to complete the camshaft drive. The new gear drive as mounted on the engine is shown with the cover removed in Figure 18. These gears are constructed of steel and are supported by ball bearings in the front cover and gear cover. The gears, which are bolted to the camshafts, have offset mounting holes to allow for different camshaft timing settings. The gear train includes

Figure 18. Cam gear drive.

provision for driving the distributor and the fuel pump.

The camshafts are held in place in the cylinder head by aluminium bearing caps that are secured by two studs. Extension of these studs provide a mounting for the cam covers. Some consideration was given to alternative gear materials in the interest of weight reduction. However, with reliability being the prime factor, our decision was to remain with steel and defer the study of other materials to future developments.

At this time I should like to give consideration to those features of the design that required an early – and, on such a small timescale, nearly irrevocable – decision as to how they would feature on the 1964 Indianapolis 500 race engine. These include the combustion chamber and its associated valving, and the piston design.

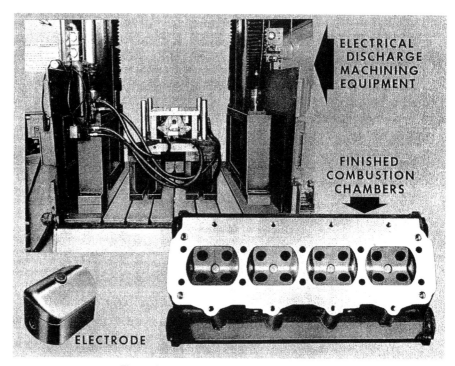

Figure 20. Combustion chamber machining.

Combustion chamber

The 'pent-roof' combustion chambers of a cylinder head are shown in Figure 19, with the four valves per place. The sparkplug is located in the centre portion of the chamber where the

Figure 19. Combustion chamber.

maximum burning efficiency can occur. When we ran into the problem of machining the combustion chambers to the close tolerances required, we turned to our manufacturing Development Group for help. They employed a technique known as Electrical Discharge Machining (EDM), or 'spark erosion' as it is sometimes known by, which is described later under Special Considerations.

It was necessary to place cylinder head mounting studs on the face of the cylinder head in addition to those on the cylinder block. This was to prevent the studs passing through the inlet and exhaust ports and complicating the cylinder head design, while still providing six bolting positions around each combustion chamber. All oil and water passages are sealed with O-rings placed in grooves in the cylinder block. As an added precaution against water leaks, the core support holes on the cylinder

head face were sealed by welding prior to cylinder head machining.

Pistons

The piston design and material were carefully selected to produce maximum strength for minimum weight (Figure 21). For this reason, the piston is an aluminium alloy extrusion. The piston pin is full floating and its length is carefully controlled to minimize the

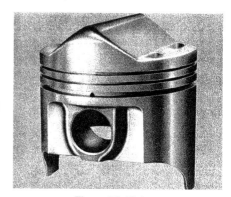

Figure 21. Piston.

impact loading on the pin retainers. The pistons were cam-ground, tapered, and fit with a clearance of 0.175-0.2mm (0.007-0.008in) in the bores.

Connecting rods

This component required a new design because of the increased loads experienced at the higher operating speeds. A comparison of the two designs is shown in Figure 22. The piston pin diameter has been increased from 23.2mm (0.914in) to 24.8mm (0.975in). It can be noted that additional material has been added to the bolt boss area of the connecting rod and cap. This was necessary to accommodate the installation of a larger diameter connecting rod bolt, and to provide

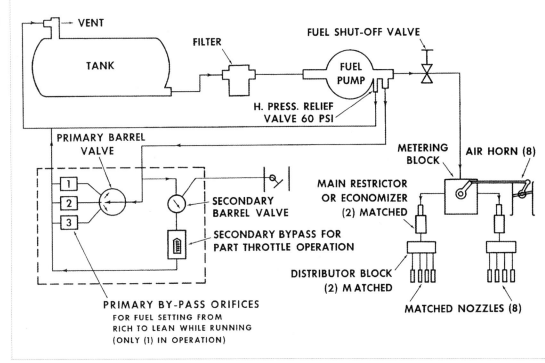

Figure 23. Fuel injection system – Indianapolis race engine.

better connecting rod bearing bore geometry control while operating at the high inertia loads in excess of 8000rpm.

The over-plated copper-lead bearings used were retained in the earlier 1964 engines, however examination of these bearings after being subjected to the higher loads developed at engine speeds in excess of 8000rpm gave clear evidence of possible failure. Accordingly, these bearings were changed to a higher hardness steel backing that can withstand unit stress in the order of 10,000psi.

Fuel injection system

This aspect of our overall engine design is critical to our attaining maximum

performance. Figure 23 shows a schematic of the system, which is basically a Hilborn; however certain significant design adaptations have been incorporated in order to meet the performance criteria that our development analysis had established. Hilborn fuel injection is widely used, however, its adoption for the Ford engine is the only instance in which it is being employed with gasoline as a fuel in the Indianapolis 500 race. In all other instances methanol or other non-gasoline/petrol fuels are employed. This is a significant difference.

The system provides a continuous fuel flow at relatively low pressure (60psi maximum line pressure at 8000rpm) with good control and a wide range of delivery capacity. Our delivery requirement of approximately 245lb of fuel per hour at 8000rpm would not tax the system. The main functioning

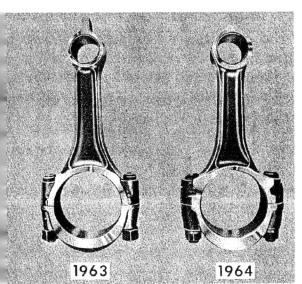

Figure 22. The connecting rod on the left is not as strong as the connecting rod on the right.

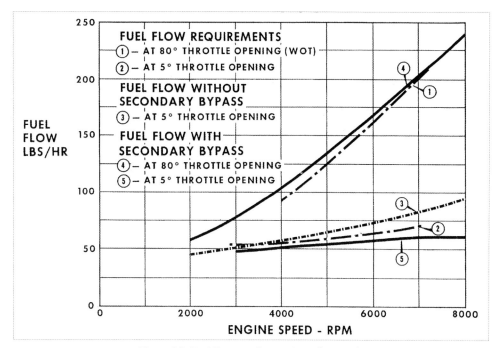

Figure 24. Fuel flow requirements and control.

elements are: the constant volume gear pump, the metering block, economizer valves (main restrictor), the by-pass orifices, together with the primary barrel valve, and the nozzles.

The constant volume gear pump is mounted on the front gear cover, and is driven at half engine speed from the camshaft. Twice the amount of fuel necessary is available at the output side of the pump. The amount actually delivered forward to the metering block is controlled by the fixed orifice by-pass, which returns a precisely predetermined amount of fuel back to the fuel tank. For this purpose, a switch (primary barrel valve) permits one of three fixed orifice bypasses to be used at any one time (1 – normal running; 2 – slightly leaner; and 3 – slightly leaner again). Orifice selection also, in effect, moves the family of curves of flow rate (pounds of fuel per hour versus engine speed in rpm) up or down, for richness or leanness.

The metering block is linked with the throttle plates and controls the fuel flow at part throttle. The two economizer valves are located between the metering block and the nozzles. Their purpose is to achieve matching in the fuel requirement curve at full throttle. This is accomplished by varying the preload and spring rate of the economizer valves to accord with the fuel flow curve (Figure 24).

Extensive wind tunnel testing was conducted with the fuel injection system, with special attention to its hot fuel handling capabilities. The tests were conducted at an air speed of 120mph and an ambient temperature of 51°C (125°F). Air speed, traction force and road speed were recorded throughout the test, as were the temperatures given by thermocouples installed at various points on the engine. For example, fuel temperatures were recorded going into and coming out of the pump and at the six vehicle

tanks. During the most severe run, the fuel temperature stabilized at a maximum of 58°C (136°F). Since the possibility of vapor lock needed to be rigorously assessed, several Ried vapor pressure determinations were made using five fuel types. No vapor locks were encountered.

Track testing during March of 1964 at the Indianapolis Speedway yielded the following refinements to the Hilborn installation:

A – Determination of the throttle linkage.
B – Incorporation of dual economizer valves to improve throttle response during tip-in.
C – Incorporation of a pressure relief valve and secondary by-pass feature to reduce manifold flooding (loading) caused by high speed close-throttle running in the corners.

Other factors bearing on achieving optimum functioning with the fuel injection

After considerable investigation, we determined that the shift in the fuel load through the equalizer liner between the left- and right-hand tanks under the influence of the acceleration forces in the turns was the cause. Once the problem had been determined, its correction was readily accomplished.

Lubrication system

In the early stages of our 1964 development programme we continued to use the oil pump system (dry-sump system) that had been developed and used on the 1963 engine. We were aware, however, that the demands imposed on the overhead camshaft

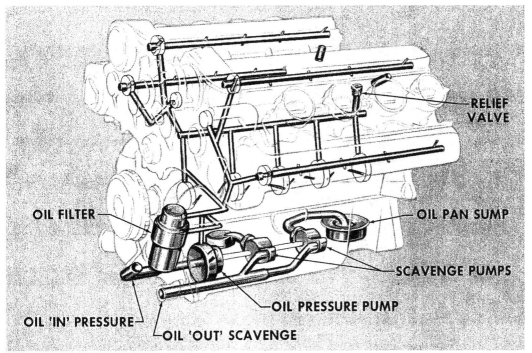

OIL FILTER

RELIEF VALVE

OIL PAN SUMP

SCAVENGE PUMPS

OIL PRESSURE PUMP

OIL 'IN' PRESSURE

OIL 'OUT' SCAVENGE

Figure 25. Lubrication system.

engine might require revisions. The 1963 system consisted of a pressure pump to supply oil to the engine, and a scavenge pump, which removed oil from the pan and gases from the crankcase and took them to a sump tank located forward in the car near to the oil cooler.

When we found it necessary to lubricate each lobe of the camshafts, the pressure pump capacity was increased. This, of course, put a greater demand on the scavenge system, not only in the quantity of oil to be handled but also in the greater tendency of the oil to foam when draining back from the overhead camshafts through the moving parts of the engine. In order to cope with the larger demand of oil and air made on the scavenge pump system we increased the scavenge pump capacity by 100% and increased the pickup tube size by 50%. This was adequate to scavenge the crankcase completely. At Indianapolis

during testing we learned that when we approached 8000rpm one of our greatest problems was throwing oil out of the breather. This appeared at Kingman also, and it later proved to be the number one problem. This oil throwing condition had two principal aspects: the oil was subjected to considerable windage by the action of the rotating crankshaft assembly; secondly, since it is necessary to circulate a large amount of oil through the engine due to the large bearing clearances required for lubrication and cooling, this results in more throw-off. In addition, the breathing system must cope with the scavenge pump pulling the air from the crankcase and various cavities within the engine into the sump tank. We have no road draft tube or outlet air system as such in the crankcase.

After we found that we solved this problem of oil throwing by increasing

the scavenge pump and intake tube size, and incorporating better baffling, we added a second scavenge pump and pickup as further assurance against either failure of the scavenge pump or its inability to handle the increased volume of gas resulting from increased blow-by in the engine. The elements of the new lubrication system included the following:

A – Redesigned oil pan baffle to control the windage created by the rotating crankshaft assembly.
B – Installation of surge baffles to prevent excessive oil in the area of the timing gears.
C – Better control of the oil to the overhead camshafts. This was accomplished by restricting the quantity of oil going to the camshaft lobes and bearings, and installing a return system that prevented the oil draining from the cylinder heads coming into contact with the rotating crankshaft assembly.
D – Increasing the capacity of the scavenge pump.
E – Installing a second scavenge pump to insure a more complete pickup of oil from the pan and scavenging of the blow-by gases from the crankcase.
F – Vented sump tank.

A low restriction oil filter was added to the front cover to remove foreign particles that seemed to be present in the tubes and connections in the sump system.

Exhaust system

It is well known that much can be done to improve engine performance by suitable tuning of the exhaust system. An exhaust system based on the theoretical tube length of 71.6in was developed on the dynamometer. It was decided to pursue a ½ and ¼ wave length study since each of these offered advantages in accommodating the system in the vehicle. Accordingly, several systems were designed using both 36in and 18in long primary pipes.

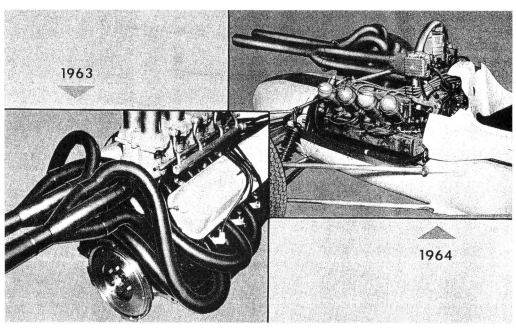

Figure 26. Exhaust comparison. The 1963 exhaust system uses 36in long primary pipes.

Figure 27. The evolution of the exhaust system.

INDIANAPOLIS 500

For the time, these DOHC V8 engines were at the 'top'; representing the best engine technology of the day, and successfully preceding all other similar four-valve per cylinder, four overhead camshaft V8 engines. These engines were, however, built for one application, which the management of Ford Division saw as important – the Indianapolis 500 race. This limited the overall usefulness of these engines in a sense, but that aside, no other engine performed better in this specific application. The much older Meyer-Drake or Offenhauser 255ci/4.2-litre four cylinder in-line engine was right there with it though, and, without a doubt, was the measure of the day at the Indianapolis Speedway.

For the record, and besides winning numerous other races on the US ovals, the DOHC Ford V8 engine powered the following winning Indianapolis 500 cars: a Lotus-Ford driven by Jim Clark in 1965; a Lotus-Ford driven by Graham Hill in 1966; a Coyote-Ford driven by AJ Foyt in 1967; a Hawk-Ford driven by Mario Andretti in 1969; and finally, a PJ Colt-Ford driven by Al Unser in 1970.

Engines after 1965 were not made by Ford. Sonny Meyer of Meyer-Drake had the rights from Ford to make these engines, and after him they passed to AJ Foyt. The suppliers Ford had contracted to make specialist componentry continued to make parts for Meyer-Drake and AJ Foyt. This meant that new engines and parts were readily available into the 1970s.

In testing, the early engines developed approximately 385bhp with petrol/gasoline and the later engines 425bhp, which is the power the engines developed for the 1964 race.

As it was, there were seven race teams equipped with DOHC Ford V8 engines in the 1964 Indianapolis 500, with Jim Clark in the Lotus taking pole position. Other DOHC Ford V8 engine users included Roger Ward, Dan Gurney, Bob Marshman, Eddie Sachs, Dave MacDonald and Eddie Johnson. On the third lap, Dave MacDonald lost control of his rear-engined Ford V8-powered Mickey Thompson-Sears Special and hit the wall. The car then bounced back, catching on fire, into the path of the American Red Ball Express Special (another rear-engined Ford V8-powered car) driven by Eddie Sachs. The two cars, full of gasoline/petrol, ignited and both drivers were unfortunately killed in this horrific accident.

The race was restarted with Jim Clark and his Lotus-Ford out in front. He held the lead until lap 48 when a collapsed left rear suspension and flat tyre meant he ended the race in the pits. The tyre tread had disintegrated far too quickly, and this problem had a knock-on affect for Dan Gurney, who was using the same tyres on a similar car to Clark. Dunlop engineers asked that he be withdrawn from the race to avoid another accident, so Gurney was called into the pits on lap 117, and the car retired.

The 1964 Indianapolis 500 race was won by AJ Foyt in a conventional Offenhauser-powered roadster, and Roger Ward finished second in a rear-engined Ford DOHC V8-powered, AJ Watson-built, Kaiser Aluminium Special.

Interestingly, the engine in Roger Ward's car was not quite what it should have been. The car pitted for fuel on about lap 30, and Ford engineers present, who knew the size of the fuel load, couldn't understand why the car needed more fuel so soon. It came into the pits for fuel no less than five times during the race, which meant a lot of time was lost. The true reason for this was only revealed after the race. The engineer on the Roger Ward car, AJ Watson, had modified the fuel injection system to run on methyl-alcohol fuel. Watson wanted to increase power and reliability by using this fuel, which had a higher latent heat of evaporation than petrol/gasoline, so the internal engine components would run cooler. Although this meant that the car required more fuel during the race than it otherwise would have. The engine modification had been made without the knowledge of the Ford engineers, or the permission of Ford management. Needless to say, this did not go down well at Ford, especially as the higher fuel consumption had likely cost this Ford-powered car the race: the engine was clearly powerful enough without the use of methyl-alcohol, and it was proven to be reliable on petrol/gasoline. Watson thought that overall his modification would give the car the best possible chance of winning, but in the end the increased fuel consumption cost the Roger Ward car the race.

All of the Ford DOHC engines had to go back to Ford after the Indianapolis race. They were stripped down and checked for component wear, rebuilt, tested, and shipped back to the respective racing teams. After doing this, Ford engineers had a very good idea of what, if anything, had gone wrong with an engine, and how the engines were fairing under harsh operating conditions.

For 1965, Ford intended to sell these engines to race teams for $25,000. It sold 50 of them at the beginning of that year to the various teams that had a total of 30 racing cars, including primary and backup cars, between them. This meant that all race teams had at least one spare engine. On average, 15-17 of these Ford V8-powered cars would qualify for a race.

The engines were modified further for 1965, with the rpm increased from the 'controlled' maximum of 8600-8800rpm to 9500-9700rpm. This meant Ford engineers had to continue the test-fail-redesign process to ensure reliable engine performance at the higher operating revs. A V8 of 4.2-litre capacity, with pistons of 95.2mm (3.750in) diameter and stroke of 73.0mm (2.875in), turning to 9700rpm with complete reliability for the length of a race such as the Indianaoplis 500 was completely unheard of in 1964-1965 before Ford. Plus, these engines were developing 505-515bhp on methyl-alcohol fuel.

While the 1963 and 1964 engines had been manufactured in the Engine Engineering building at the Ford Engine Centre in Dearborn, the 50 DOHC 1965 engines were assembled at the Ford Rouge complex in the Engine Quality Control building adjacent to the Dearborn Engine Plant, which was where the 'FE' V8 engines were all made. There were six people in the building working on this engine project, and seven engineers from the Indy Engine Group visited the facility on a very regular basis to check progress and discuss material deviations resulting from inspections. Each completed engine was 'hot-tested' on site at no load for about three to five minutes to check oil pressure and any signs of water or oil leaks. The hot-tested engines were then sent to the EEE building. Here they were 'run in' on Ford's GE dynamometer for 20 minutes then tested for maximum torque and brake horsepower, up to 9700rpm. In order to test the engines as high as 9700rpm, the rpm limiting function was removed from the GE engine dynamometer. The GE calibration engineers, who regularly

checked the dynamometer, knew what the Ford engineers were doing. They warned that the electronics could shut down at this amount of rpm and the engine would be a 'run away,' which would see the engine disintegrate, and possibly wreck the dynamometer. This 'run away' situation did in fact occur a couple of times and the ignition had to be cut very quickly by the ever vigilant dynamometer operators, who had a hand on the emergency stop button at all times!

The 1965 Indianapolis 500 race saw no mistakes, and Jim Clark won in record time with a naturally-aspirated methyl-alcohol burning DOHC Ford V8 engined Lotus-Ford. After a Ford-powered car won the Memorial Day race, Ford management stopped the whole project, and the Indy Engine Group was disbanded and reassigned new work.

The 1966 and 1967 Indianapolis 500 winning cars were powered by Ford's naturally-aspirated, alcohol burning engine; the Lotus-Ford driven by Graham Hill, and the Coyote-Ford by AJ Foyt, respectively. The 1968 winner was powered by a turbocharged Offenhauser engine.

Ford no longer had any official involvement with Indy car racing, but Ford engineers did on occasion assist in a private capacity, such as when asked by Sonny Mayer. For example, in late 1968 Mayer sought advice on how to reduce engine capacity from 4.2-litres/255ci to 2.6-litres/156ci in preparation for turbo-charging. In this instance, a new crankshaft was designed by Ford Engine engineer Bill Barr in his own time. The compression ratio was approximately 8.0:1, and these turbocharged 2.6-litre Ford V8 engines reportedly produced 1100bhp and turned to 11,200rpm.

The 1969 race was won by Mario Andretti in a Hawk-Ford with a turbocharged alcohol burning version of the DOHC Ford V8 engine. Al Unser won the Indianapolis 500 in 1970 and 1971 driving a PJ Colt-Ford with a similar specification turbocharged alcohol burning DOHC Ford V8 engine. From 1969 to 1971 the turbocharged alcohol burning DOHC Ford V8 engines powered over 75% of the winning cars.

OTHER APPLICATIONS FOR THE INDY ENGINE

The small block derived DOHC Indy Ford V8 engine was used in Formula One in 1966 by Bruce McLaren, who received four engines from Ford. Capacity was reduced to 3.0-litre via bore and stroke reductions, and it underwent a whole host of other changes under direction of Klaus Von Rucker, the well-known German automobile engine designer, to make it suitable for this application. However, it didn't prove to be all that successful, and the engine lacked the necessary wide torque band, despite sounding amazingly good!

The same powerplant appeared in a twin-engined dragster, in the USA in the '60s. With one DOHC V8 engine behind the other, it was an extremely well-engineered car, but it didn't perform as well as expected.

Finally, an enthusiast more-or-less bolted a DOHC unit straight into a GT-40 (in place of the pushrod operated unit found in all other GT-40s) in the '80s, filling the engine bay.

Without doubt, the DOHC Indianapolis 500 Ford V8 preceded all others of the type, and was the world's first highly successful four-valve per cylinder, four overhead camshaft V8 racing engine.

Chapter 7
Ford publication – 1965 Indianapolis V8 DOHC Engine

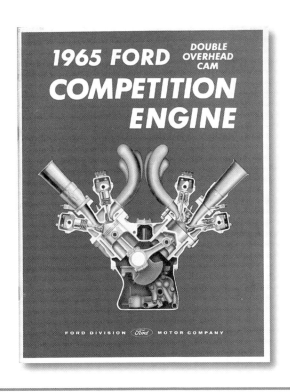

THE 1965 FORD
DOUBLE OVERHEAD CAM
COMPETITION ENGINE

Produced by
Ford Division
Ford Motor Company
Dearborn, Michigan

INTRODUCTION

In recognition of the fact that Ford double overhead cam competition engines require special care and handling to fully realize the high-performance characteristics built into them, this manual has been prepared as a practical guide for specific adjustment, maintenance, and repair procedures.

Included are specifications, torque values, fit and clearance dimensions, installation diagrams, general descriptions of systems and components, adjustments, and the use of special tools.

Particular care by the Ford Engine and Foundry Division to establish the use of special materials which provide extreme durability and reliability throughout the life of each engine has also established the necessity for certain precautions not normally observed with conventional engines. Therefore, particular attention must be given to inspection and cleanliness of parts, torque values, and tightening sequences for the cylinder heads and various engine covers. It is strongly recommended that the service instructions contained herein be rigidly adhered to in order to provide the optimum in power and performance.

This manual is intended for the owner and experienced technicians who understand the standard procedures and precautions necessary to successfully prepare precision equipment for competition, rather than an elementary guide to the complete step-by-step overhaul procedures.

Figure 1 – The 1965 Ford Double Overhead Cam Competition Engine

GENERAL DESCRIPTION

The Ford double overhead cam competition engines are lightweight, high-speed, water-cooled power units which can be operated on a variety of fuels.

The same basic cylinder block design as used in production engines has evolved into this all-aluminum block with centrifucally-cast iron cylinder lines. The materials used in manufacture, the pent-roof combustion chambers, and the over-head cam design are, of course, unique in the design of this competition-type engine. Also, in the area of engine lubrication, the dry sump principle is utilized for increased capacity and additional road clearance. Components which are subjected to high unit stresses, impact loading, or exposure to extreme operational environments have also been strengthened by the use of special materials or by redesign.

The fuel system is an adaptation of a proven injection system, and it is able to successfully use methanol or gasoline, if so desired, with a relatively minor conversion operation.

The induction and exhaust configurations available are an asset in the installation of the Ford D.O.H.C. engine in many chassis designs.

The cooling system of the engine features an attached water pump which is designed to deliver approximately 92 gpm at 8000 rpm. This will prove adequate for most well-engineered radiator or cooler installations.

The Ford D.O.H.C. breakerless transistor ignition system provides compactness and high reliability. The circuit permits a spark coil to deliver an almost constant voltage throughout the entire high speed range. Three types of Autolite spark plugs are available to meet varying conditions of operation. The Autolite AG-603 with an internal tip racing-type gap and the AG-701 with a standard gap. Either are recommended for long-distance running due to the cold heat range. The Autolite AG-901 with a standard gap is a hotter plug, and recommended for events of 100 miles or less.

Figure 2 – Lotus Car Powered with Ford D.O.H.C. Engine

1

GENERAL DATA
Specifications

Displacement	255.118 Maximum	Valve Gage Diameter	
Bore	3.7600 - 3.7595	Exhaust	1.36
Stroke	2.872 - 2.868	Intake	1.46
Compression Ratio	12.0:1 - 12.5:1		
Volume Controlling Compression Ratio	45.5 - 47.5 cc	Valve Lash (Engine Cold or Hot)	
		Exhaust	.017 — .019
Cylinder Head Combustion Chamber Volume with Plugs and Valves Installed	84.5 - 85.5 cc	Intake	.014 — .016
Block and Piston Negative Combustion Chamber Volume for Head Sealing Ring	38.0 - 39.0 cc	Engine Weight	
		Dry (Without Exhaust Tubes)	400 lbs.
Cylinder Bore Numbering Method-			
Right Bank (from front)	1-2-3-4	Spark Advance	47° Max. at 2000 rpm (Methanol) 51° Max. at 2000 rpm (Gasoline)
Left Bank (from front)	5-6-7-8		
		Idle Speed Setting	1500 rpm

Minimum Compression Pressure With All Spark Plugs Removed Maximum-to-Minimum Cylinder Pressures Must Not Exceed 20 PSI at RPM Tested

	200 RPM	235 PSI	Oil	ESE-M2C99-A
	300 RPM	242 PSI		
	400 RPM	249 PSI	Valve Arrangement per cylinder	Two intake valves outboard Two exhaust valves inboard
	500 RPM	256 PSI		
	600 RPM	263 PSI		
	700 RPM	270 PSI	Valve Seat Width	
	800 RPM	277 PSI	Exhaust	.06 — .07
	900 RPM	283 PSI	Intake	.05 — .06
	1000 RPM	289 PSI	Valve Seat Angle	
Firing Order	1-5-4-2-6-3-7-8	Exhaust	45°
Oil Pressure	50 psi Minimum @ 2000 rpm & 170° F Oil	Intake	45°

Engine Balancing

Weights of Reciprocating Parts	Grams	Weights of Rotating Parts	
		Big end of Conn. Rod (2)	1092 ± 2
Piston (1)	591 ± 1	Crank Pin Bearing	98
		Oil in Crankpin	14
Rings (Total Compression and Oil - 1 set)	39	Total Weight	1204 ± 2
Piston Pin (1)	159.5 ± 1.5	Bobweights for Crank Pins	2194
Piston Pin Retainers (2)	4	Static Balance of Assemblies	
		Vibration Damper (No CWT)	No Unbalance
Piston Pin End of Conn. Rod	197 ± 1	Flywheel (No CWT)	No Unbalance
Total Weight	990.5 ± 3.5	Mass Balance of Engine *(if engine is firing, speed must be 2000-2400 rpm)	00 ± .5 oz. in.

*After mass balancing of engine assembly, the amount and location of unbalance is etched on the crankshaft damper. The unbalance is given in ounce-inches, measured from the "0" timing mark when looking into the clutch face.

2

GENERAL DATA
Fits and Clearances

	INTERFERENCE	CLEARANCE
CYLINDER BLOCK		
Sleeve to Block		
Sleeve Body to Block	.004–.001	
Sleeve Shoulder to Block C'bore		.006–.000
Main Bearing Journal Thrust		
Face Runout	.001	
Idler Shaft Bearing to Block	.0020–.0007	
CYLINDER HEADS		
Valve Guide to Guide Bore	.002–.001	
Valve Seat Insert to Insert Bore	.0055–.0035	
Valve Spring Lower Seat to Valve Guide		.010–.001
Valve Stem to Valve Guide		
Exhaust		.0020–.0035
Intake		.0015–.0030
Valve Spring Installed Height		
(Outer Spring)		1.80 ± .020
Camshaft Journal to Cap		.0033–.0015
Camshaft End Play		.0074–.0034
Tappet to Tappet Bore		.0039–.0024
PISTON RINGS AND RODS		
Piston to Cylinder Bore (Diametrical)		.0080–.0065
Piston Land to Bore		.0300–.0255
Piston Skirt to Bore		.0065–.0080
Top of Piston to Head		.050–.035
Piston Flat Below Top of Block		.046–.035
Piston Pin to Piston		.0009–.0005
Piston Pin to Rod		.0009–.0005
Piston Pin to Retainer End Play		.001–.025
Side Clearance of Rods (Total 2 Rods)		.024–.014
Piston Rings		
Vertical Clearance - Compression Ring (Top)		.0035–.0020
Vertical Clearance - Oil Ring		.0065–.0005
Piston Ring Gaps		
(Checked in Cylinder Bore)		
Compression Rings		.035–.025
Oil Rings		.065–.025

3

GENERAL DATA
Fits and Clearances – cont'd

	INTERFERENCE	CLEARANCE
GEAR DRIVE		
Gear Backlash (4 places - 90° Apart)		.003-.007
Gear End Play*(Int. Drive-to-Cam Drive)		.003-.016
Idler Gear Shaft-to-Intermediate Idler Drive Gear Shaft Hole		.000-.001
Gear End Play*(Int. Idler-to-Idler Drive)		.005-.020
Cam Gear-to-Cam Post		.001-.003
Shafts-to-Roller Bearings (Except Int. Idler Drive Gear Assembly)		.0001-.0010
Shafts-to-Roller Bearings (Int. Idler Drive Gear Assembly)		.0005–.0015
CRANKSHAFT		
Crankshaft End Play		.004-.008
Runout of Flywheel Face at Clutch Periphery after Assembly to Crankshaft		.0015
Pilot Bearing-to-Crankshaft	.0015-.0000	
Crankshaft Main Journals and Bearing (Select-Fit)		.0030-.0020
Crankshaft Pin Journals and Bearing (Select-Fit)		.0032-.0026
OIL SYSTEM		
Oil Pump (Pressure)		
Drive Gear Backlash		.003-.007
Drive Gear-to-Drive Shaft	.0000-.0008	
Pump Gear-to-Drive Shaft	.0005-.0013	
Drive Shaft-to-Bearing Cap		.0015-.0027
Drive Shaft-to-Pump Housing		.0011-.0023
Pump Gear End Play		.0032-.0062
Driven Gear-to-Driven Shaft	.0011-.0020	
Driven Shaft-to-Bearing Cap		.0015-.0027
Driven Shaft-to-Pump Housing		.0012-.0022
Driven Gear End Play		.0032-.0062
Oil Pump (Scavenge - Front and Rear)		
Pump Gear-to-Drive Shaft	.0005-.0013	
Drive Shaft-to-Bearing Cap		.0015-.0027
Drive Shaft-to-Pump Housing		.0010-.0023
Drive Gear End Play		.0032-.0062
Driven Gear-to-Driven Shaft	.0005-.0013	
Driven Shaft-to-Bearing Cap		.0015-.0027
Driven Shaft-to-Pump Housing		.0010–.0023
Driven Gear End Play		.0032-.0062
COOLING SYSTEM		
Impeller-to-Water Pump Shaft	.0012-.0022	
Shaft Bearing in Housing	.0015-.0028	
Pump Seal in Housing	.002-.007	
Slinger on Pump Shaft	.0012-.0047	
Impeller Vane to Housing		.013-.023
Pump Housing in Front Cover	.001-.000	
Drive Gear on Pump Shaft	.0014-.0024	
Drive Gear Backlash-to-Crankshaft Gear		.003-.007

*Shim gear cover bearings or grind gear shoulders as required.

4

GENERAL DATA
Torque Specifications

OPERATION	THREAD SIZE	INSTALLATION TORQUE
Clamp - Water By-pass Hose		15 – 20 in. lb.
Nut - Connecting Rod (Hand Start-Hand Torque)	13/32 – 24	45 – 50 ft. lb.
Bolt - Pressure Plate-to-Flywheel	5/16 – 18	12 – 20 ft. lb.
Bolt - Flywheel-to-Crankshaft	7/16 – 20	75 – 85 ft. lb.
Plug - Oil Pan Drain	1 – 12	15 – 20 ft. lb.
Bolt - Crankshaft Damper-to-Crankshaft	5/8 – 18	100 – 120 ft. lb.
Spark Plug (Wire-Brush & Spray Threads With Graphite)	14 MM	15 – 25 ft. lb.
Bolt - Exhaust Manifold-to-Cylinder Head	3/8 – 16 5/16 – 18	20 – 25 ft. lb. 12 – 15 ft. lb.
Bolt - Front Cover-to-Cylinder Head	1/4 – 20	84 – 96 in. lb.
Bolt - Distributor Hold-Down	5/16 – 18	12 – 15 ft. lb.
Bolt - Main Bearing Cap	3/8 – 16 3/8 – 24 7/16 – 14	25 – 35 ft. lb. 25 – 35 ft. lb. 70 – 80 ft. lb.
Nut - Cam Tower Cover	1/4 – 28	25 – 35 in. lb.
Bolt - Camshaft Bearing Caps	1/4 – 28 5/16 – 24	6 – 9 ft. lb. 15 – 18 ft. lb.
Bolt - Oil Pan-to-Block	5/16 – 18	9 – 11 ft. lb.
Nut - Oil Filter Element		Finger Tight
Nut - Oil Filter Element-Lock	3/8 – 16	25 – 30 in. lb.
Nut - Oil Filter Housing	3/8 – 16	10 – 12 ft. lb.
Bolt - Gear Cover-to-Front Cover Clamp	1/4 – 20	25 – 30 in. lb.
Nut - Rear Main Bearing Cap	1/2 – 13	75 – 85 ft. lb.
Distributor Cap Hold Down Screws		9 – 10 in. lb.

Engine Assembly Turning Torque -
  Crank and Pistons Installed
  Complete Engine Less Spark Plugs
		25 – 35 ft. lb.
		60 – 75 ft. lb.

The following general installation torque specifications apply to any operation not listed above.

THREAD SIZE	TORQUE FT. - LB.	THREAD SIZE	TORQUE FT. - LB.
1/4'' – 20	6 – 9	7/16'' – 14	45 – 50
1/4'' – 28	6 – 9	7/16'' – 20	50 – 60
1/4'' Pipe	12 – 17	1/2'' – 13	60 – 70
5/16'' – 18	12 – 15	1/2'' – 20	70 – 80
5/16'' – 24	15 – 18	1/2'' Pipe	70 – 80
3/8'' – 16	20 – 25	9/16'' – 18	85 – 95
3/8'' – 24	28 – 37	5/8'' – 18	130 – 145
3/8'' Pipe	23 – 28	3/4'' Pipe	130 – 145

5

INSTALLATION

Prior to shipment the engine, attached pumps, and other rotating components were carefully tested individually and in combination as complete units. In addition, the engine has been evaluated on the hot test stand before preparation for shipment as follows:

o The correct lubricating oil and fuel were used.
o The ignition wires were protected for distressing heat.
o The crankcase oil was heated to 140° F before the engine was started. A

maximum operating temperature of 210° F was maintained.
o The coolant was heated to 140° F before the engine was started. The operating range was 160-170° F.
o Spark advance was set to specification and the retard switch on the ignition was used for starting.
o The oil pressure was 50 psi minimum within 30 seconds.
o The engine was operated 10 minutes at 2000 rpm, 5 minutes at 3000 rpm, and 5 minutes at 4000 rpm for a total of 20 minutes at no load.

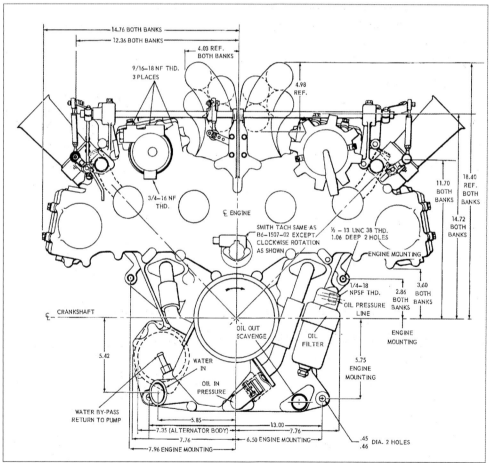

Figure 3 – Front View of Engine

6

INSTALLATION

o The engine was mass-balanced to specifications.

o Gasket areas, cast surfaces, and bolt attachments were examined externally for leaks, and the leaks corrected.

o The engine oil and coolant were drained. Drain plugs were installed and safety-wired.

After the hot test, the following inspections were made:

o Cylinder bores.
o Cam lobes and tappets.
o Valve lash.
o Connecting rod bearings.
o Number 4 and 5 main bearings.
o Oil pan and filter.

o Main and connecting rod bearing cap nuts specified torque.

o External gasket flanges and safety wire.

Before shipment, the engine was "fogged" to prevent corrosion during storage. All exposed components sensitive to dirt were covered, and all open holes plugged or capped. All units were ready for immediate service following a final check after installation.

The following engineering drawings will assist in the installation of the Ford D.O.H.C. engine as well as a guide for the dimensions of mounting brackets for additional customizing components.

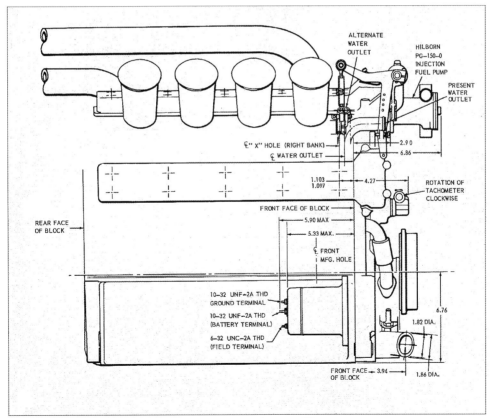

Figure 4 – Right Side View of Engine

7

INSTALLATION

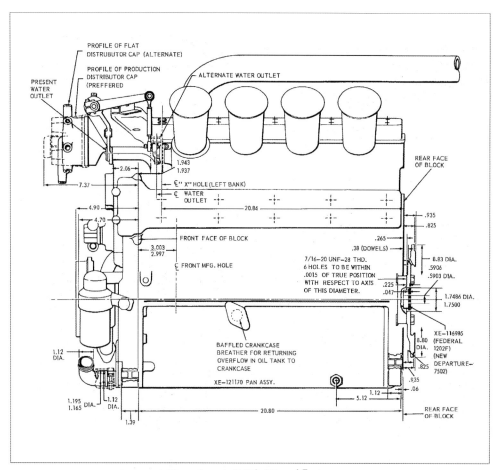

Figure 5 — Left Side View of Engine

8

INSTALLATION

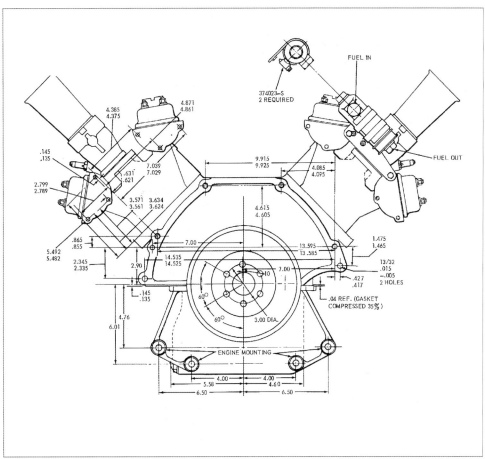

Figure 6 — Rear View of Engine

9

THE BASIC ENGINE

Cylinder Block

The Ford competition engines have an all-aluminum alloy cylinder block with design features of the highly successful Ford 289-cubic-inch regular production cast iron engines. This basic block design was selected as most suited to meet the Indianapolis displacement requirement. In addition, the use of this basic design eliminated the necessity for a complete development program on earlier Indy engines, and it also enabled Ford to make significant improvements for the 1965 units.

Crankshaft

The crankshaft is a forging made from aircraft quality electric furnace SAE 4340 alloy steel. The crank is carried in five main bearings that are steel-backed copper-lead with a lead-tin overlay. Torsional vibration is controlled through the use of a damper at the forward end of the crankshaft and it effectively damps torsional vibrations at speeds up to 9000 rpm.

Pistons and Connecting Rods

The pistons are aluminum extrusions of silicon-aluminum alloy, cam ground, tapered, and fit with .0065 to .0080 diametral clearance between the piston skirt in the bore. Piston pins are full floating and the lengths are carefully controlled to minimize impact loading on the pin retainers. Two compression and one oil control ring are used per piston.

Connecting rods are of new design for the 1965 engines. The rods are forgings of SAE 4340 steel which has been heat treated to a Brinell hardness of 229 - 285, magnafluxed, then polished in part. Rod bearings are steel-backed overplated copper-lead.

Cylinder Liners

Cylinder liners are exceptionally high quality centrifugally-cast iron. The liners are pressed into the cylinder block, then both the liners and block are relieved at the bottom to provide clearance for the connecting rod aircraft-type nuts during shaft rotation.

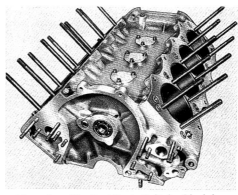

Figure 7 – The Ford Basic Cylinder Block for Competition Engines

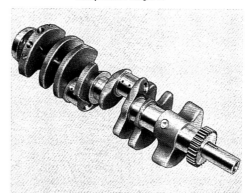

Figure 8 – The Ford Crankshaft for Competition Engines

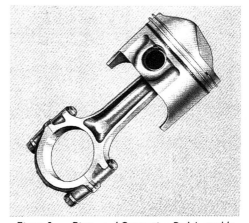

Figure 9 – Piston and Connecting Rod Assembly for the Ford D.O.H.C. Engine

10

THE BASIC ENGINE

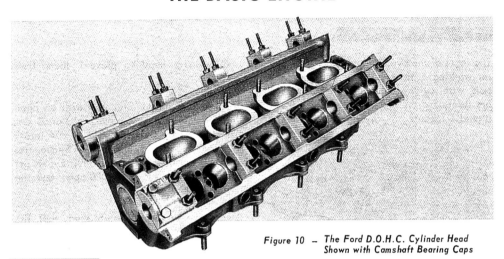

Figure 10 — The Ford D.O.H.C. Cylinder Head
Shown with Camshaft Bearing Caps

Cylinder Heads

The aluminum alloy cylinder heads are one-piece castings with combustion chambers precision-finished by "Electrical Discharge Machining." Two intake and two exhaust valves are used for each cylinder, and the spark plug is in the center of each combustion chamber to provide maximum fuel burning efficiency. Through the electrical discharge machining method, combustion chamber volume is controlled to a fraction of a cubic centimeter. The piston heads and the pent-roof combustion chambers provide efficient combustion with a compression ratio of 12.0:1 - 12.5:1.

Figure 11 — The Pent-Roof Combustion Chambers of the Ford D.O.H.C. Competition Engine

The unique design of the cylinder heads provides ports that are unrestricted by mounting studs that would complicate the basic design. The heads are each attached to the block by ten studs from the block-to-head and eight studs from head-to-block. The water and oil passages between the head and block are sealed with synthetic rubber "O" rings which are seated in grooves in the block. Also, as a further precaution against water leaks, the core support plugs on the cylinder head face are welded before machining. Cylinder-to-combustion chamber sealing is effectively accomplished by laminated stainless steel "O" rings.

The lower half of the camshaft bearing surfaces are machined in the aluminum head casting. Bearing caps are of the same material, and are secured to the heads on the studs that are used for the installation of the cam tower covers. The camshaft bearings are pressure-lubricated from oil galleries at the front of the engine, and restrictors in the galleries meter the flow of oil to the camshaft bearings and cam lobes.

Valve guides are aluminum-bronze alloy, pressed into the heads. Valve seat inserts are made of stellite for extra durability.

11

THE BASIC ENGINE

Camshafts, Tappets and Valves

The lobes of the overhead cams are designed for working against cup-type follower tappets with cylindrical surfaces. Camshafts are steel, and the tappets are steel chromeplated. Tappets are keyed to fit grooves in the cylinder head to prevent them from rotating.

Dual valve springs are used with an open load of 360 lbs. and a closed load of 95 lbs. The two springs have a .012 $\pm$ .004 interference for damping, and natural frequencies between springs differ by 5000 cycles per minute. The outer is 28,000 cpm, and the inner 33,000 cpm.

Dynamometer testing established that the best overall horsepower and torque characteristics are obtained with a total valve opening event of 306° and an 87° overlap. This requires a valve lash of .015 for intake valves and .018 for the exhaust. There is no mechanical valve lash adjustment. Valve lash is adjusted by selecting tappets with the proper head thickness.

Through careful calculation and dynamometer testing, valve gage diameter of 1.46 for the intake and 1.36 for the exhaust valve, each with a .44 lift, were determined. Figure 14 shows some of the details of the port and valve design.

Figure 12 – *Valve Tappets are Keyed to Grooves in the Cylinder Head to Prevent Them from Rotating*

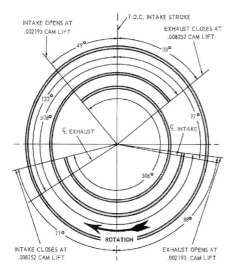

Figure 13 – *Timing Cycle for the Ford D.O.H.C. Engine*

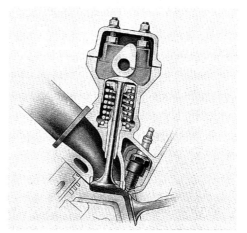

Figure 14 – *Port and Valve Detail*

12

THE BASIC ENGINE

Figure 15 – The Camshaft and Accessory Drive Gear Train for the Ford D.O.H.C. Engine

Camshaft and Accessory Drive

The camshafts, water and oil pumps, as well as the distributor, fuel pump, and alternator are driven from the gear train at the front of the engine. Steel spur gears are used throughout. Idler gears are straddle-mounted by ball bearings in the engine front cover and gear cover. The crankshaft gear is heated to 400° F, then pressed on the shaft and a steel key is used for positive location of the gear hub on the crank. Camshaft drive gears are bolted-on and have multiple mounting holes to provide a vernier adjustment for variable camshaft timing. The camshaft drive gears, as shown in Figure 15, would not normally be installed until the gear cover was assembled to the engine and gear backlash checked.

Timing Marks

Timing marks are stamped on the vibration damper on the front of the crankshaft. A pointer on the engine cover indicates TDC and other markings on the damper. Duplicate timing marks appear on the flywheel, and may be used if engine installation permits.

Figure 16 – Timing Marks for the Ford D.O.H.C. Engine

13

ENGINE SYSTEMS

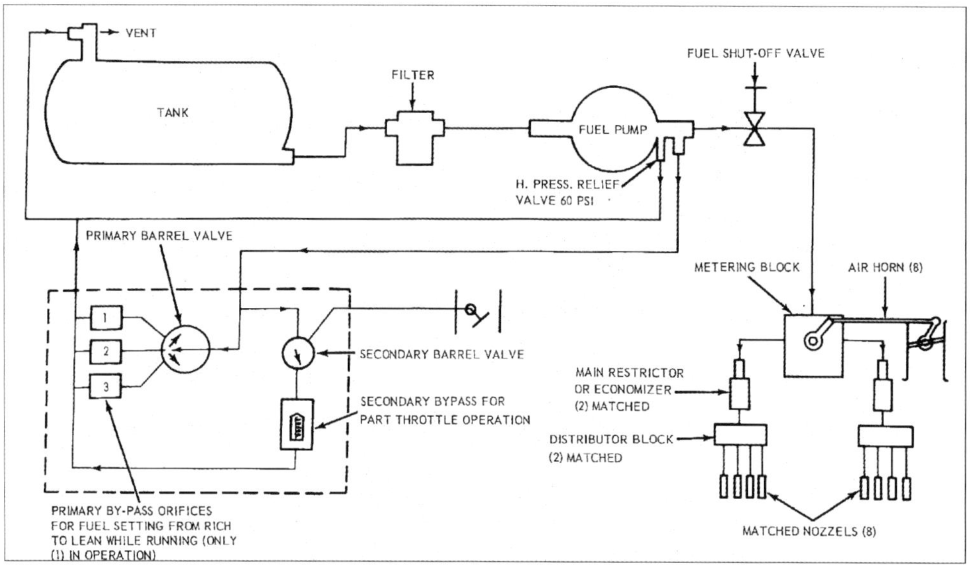

Figure 17 — Schematic Diagram of Fuel System

The Fuel System

Figure 17 shows a schematic diagram of the fuel system. Significant design adaptations have been incorporated in this Hilborn-type system to meet the performance requirements established by the development analyses of the engine. This type of system is widely used, however, the Ford D.O.H.C. engine can employ gasoline, methanol, or other non-gasoline fuels with only a relatively minor revision to the system.

The main components of the system include the constant-volume gear-type pump, metering block, economizer valves, by-pass orifices, primary barrel valve, and the matched nozzles.

The constant-volume gear-type pump is mounted on the front gear cover, and is driven at one-half engine speed by the camshaft gear. During operation, the pump will actually discharge twice the amount of fuel required for any operating condition. The amount of fuel delivered to the metering block is controlled by the fixed-orifice by-pass, which returns a precisely predetermined amount of fuel back to the tank. The primary barrel valve is the "switch" which permits selection of one of three fixed orifice by-passes. This feature enables the flow rate (pounds of fuel per hour versus engine speed) to be moved up or down for rich or lean fuel injection.

The metering block and secondary barrel valve are linked with the throttle plates to control the fuel at part throttle. Improved fuel atomization for the 1965 Ford D.O.H.C. engine is achieved with booster venturis installed in the throttle bodies. This reduces fuel requirements, and improves the performance and response of the engine.

The two economizer valves between the metering block and the nozzles maintain the balance of fuel delivery in accordance with the established fuel flow curve. The dual economizer valve installation also helps to improve throttle response during tip-in.

14

ENGINE SYSTEMS

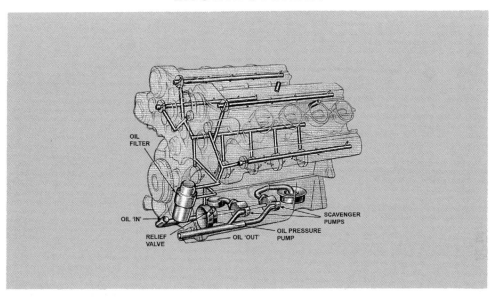

OIL
FILTER

OIL 'IN'

RELIEF
VALVE

OIL 'OUT'

OIL PRESSURE
PUMP

SCAVENGER
PUMPS

Figure 18 — Schematic Diagram of Lubrication System

Engine Lubrication

The 1965 Ford D.O.H.C. engines are equipped with a lubrication system vastly improved over previous models. All main and connecting rod bearings, as well as the camshaft bearings and cam lobes are pressure-lubricated.

The system shown in Figure 18 functions on the dry-sump principle with an oil pressure pump and two scavenge pumps. The pump covers are integral with the main bearing caps for compactness, and the pumps operate in tandem through interconnecting shafts which are driven at .727 engine speed by the water pump gear. The second scavenge pump is required because of the increased lubricating capacity of the 1965 engine. This provides a more complete pickup of oil from the pan and more effective scavenging of blow-by gases from the crankcase. The oil pan baffle is of new design to

better control the windage created by the crankshaft and rotating parts.

Control of oil flow to the overhead camshafts is accomplished by the use of restrictors in the oil galleries to the cams. The return system to the crankcase is designed to help prevent oil draining from the cylinder heads being whipped by the rotating parts.

A relief valve in the pressure pump helps prevent excessively high pressure during engine warm-up. A wafer-type, full-flow oil filter of low-restriction properties has been incorporated in the system to help minimize the detrimental effects of foreign particles in the oil. However, the filter does not eliminate the necessity for maintaining extreme cleanliness of the oil sump, lines, and other chassis fittings.

15

ENGINE SYSTEMS

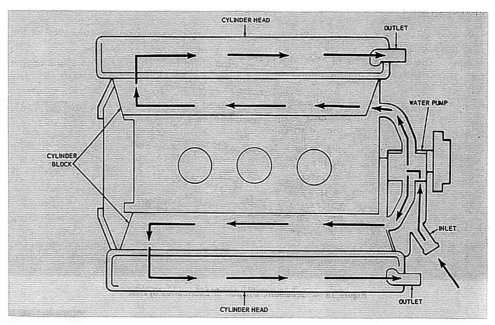

Figure 19 - Schematic Diagram of Cooling System

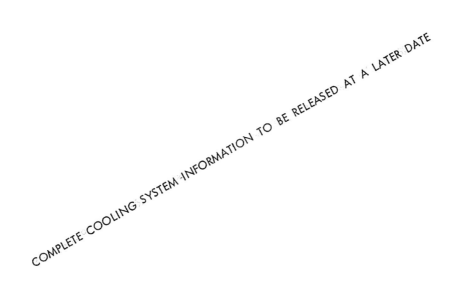

ENGINE SYSTEMS

Ignition System

The Ford breakerless ignition system was used as early as 1963 for the Ford Indianapolis engines. The higher speeds of 1964 also resulted in satisfactory operation of this unique system. For the 1965 D.O.H.C. engine, certain design refinements were made primarily in the mechanical elements and external configuration of the distributor.

Often, small innovations make a large improvement in engine performance. For instance, the addition of an anti-skid gasket has practically eliminated the possibility of the cap being dislocated as a result of vibration during high-speed runs. Also, the distributor cap is retained by a clamp and screw arrangement to help maintain positive location. The distributor drive shaft (from the left bank intake cam drive gear has been lengthened to increase the tolerance of the drive shaft concentricity.

The operational characteristics of the engine eliminate the need for a spark advance mechanism. Spark requirements, as determined by dynamometer testing, have established a fixed advance of 51° BTDC for the use of gasoline and 47° BTDC for methanol at speeds above 2000 rpm. A spark retard device is used for starting purposes.

The engine specified idle speed of 1500 rpm is, of course, at the discretion of the driver; because each driver desires a slightly different "feel" of engine responses when operating from closed-to-open throttle in the turns. In certain cases, due to operating conditions, idle speed may be as high as 2500 rpm.

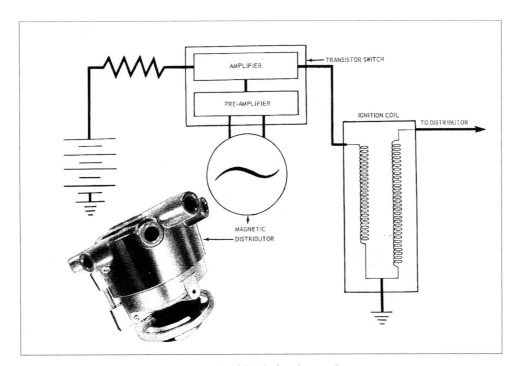

Figure 20 — Ford Breakerless Ignition System

17

MAINTENANCE

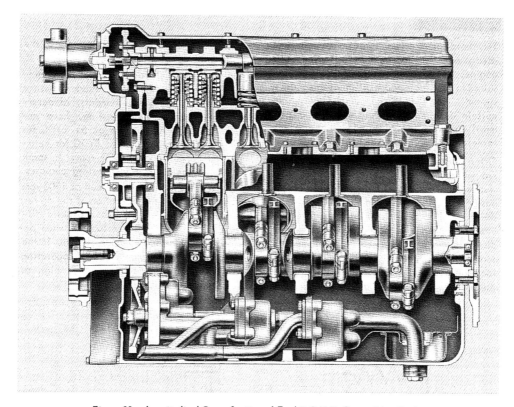

Figure 21 – Longitudinal Cross Section of Ford D.O.H.C. Competition Engine

Whenever any internal adjustment is required on the Ford D.O.H.C. competition engine or whenever fuel, oil, or coolant lines must be disconnected, extreme care must be exercised to prevent the entry of dirt or foreign particles into the engine or system. Cap or plug the lines and connections and maintain strict cleanliness in the work area.

The use of lint-free wiping materials and solvents which do not leave a residue are strongly recommended. Compressed air may be used to dry disassembled parts, after which they should be lubricated to prevent corrosion.

Precision adjustments are required to realize peak performance from the Ford D.O.H.C. competition engine, therefore, the specified fits and clearances, torque values, and tightening sequences must be adhered to. In addition, safety wire that has been removed must be installed before the engine is returned to service.

18

MAINTENANCE

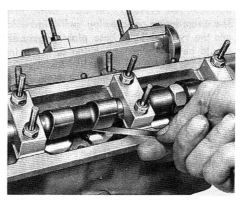

Figure 22 – Method of Checking Valve Lash

Valves and Tappets

At the time of initial engine build-up, the valves and tappets were selected for matched sets. They cannot be intermixed or the specified valve lash cannot be obtained.

The valve lash is measured between the heel of the cam and the head of the tappet. While making preliminary valve lash checks before the cylinder head is installed, the camshaft opposite to the one being checked must be in the unloaded position or removed from the head. This also applies if the head is installed on the engine and the cam drive gear is removed. If it is necessary to adjust the valve lash; remove the camshaft and select a tappet of the correct thickness to achieve the specified lash.

Valve spring height is controlled by the thickness of the valve spring lower seat. Over- and undersize spring lower seats are available to bring springs to the specified height.

Valve springs are color-coded for size and, if disassembled, must be reinstalled in sets of matching colors for selected interference. Interchanging may result in breakage or unsatisfactory spring operation.

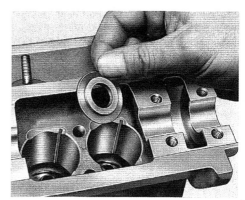

Figure 23 – Valve Spring Lower Seats are Selected to Provide the Specified Valve Spring Height

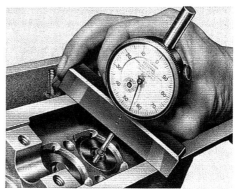

Figure 24 – Method of Checking Valve Spring Height

19

MAINTENANCE

Valves and Tappets – Cont'd.

The valve spring compressing tool (Figure 26) and the cylinder head base plate (Figure 27) should be used when removing or replacing valve and spring assemblies. The plate is bolted to the bottom of the head to keep the valves in a closed position, and the compress-ing unit lowers the spring to allow removal or installation of the valve retainers.

The tool shown in Figure 28 is used to install the valve stem seals.

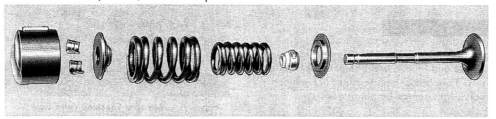

Figure 25 – Disassembled View of Valve, Springs, and Tappet

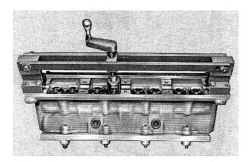

Figure 26 – Valve Spring Compressing Tool

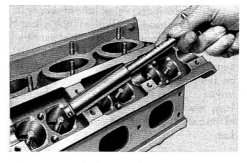

Figure 28 – Valve Stem Seal Installation

Camshaft Timing

Intake and exhaust timing is checked at No. 1 (right bank) and No. 6 (left bank).

Remove No. 1 spark plug, then use a dial indicator with a probe through the spark plug hole and turn the crankshaft to obtain No. 1 TDC.

Install the degree wheel and pointer shown in Figure 29. Set the wheel at zero to indicate TDC.

Install a dial indicator with the foot of the probe on the flat section of a tappet for No. 1 cylinder.

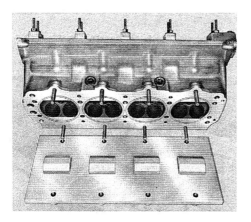

Figure 27 – Cylinder Head Base Plate

(continued next page)

20

MAINTENANCE

Turn the crankshaft clockwise from No. 1 cam lobe base circle to determine the crankshaft angle at .100 valve lift opening. If the .100 lift is not to specifications, set the crank at 11-9 degrees BTDC when checking the intake cams or 5.5-7.5 degrees BTDC when checking the exhaust cams. To correct the cam timing, loosen the camshaft gear retaining bolts, hold the cam with a wrench on the flats provided on the shaft, then turn the cam until a .100 reading is obtained on the indicator. Tighten the cam gear bolts.

Recheck the .100 lift point, then tighten cam gear bolts to specifications and install safety *wire*.

WARNING – Advancing the intake camshafts three crankshaft degrees or retarding the exhaust camshafts 12 crankshaft degrees more than specifications may result in contact between the valves and piston.

Figure 29 – Crankshaft Degree Wheel and Dial Indicator Installed for Timing Camshaft

New Camshaft Installation

The following procedure should be used when installing new camshafts or during engine overhaul.

Inspect the camshaft oil passages for foreign material. Remove the plug and snap ring from the rear of the cam and introduce oil or sol-

vent under pressure. Observe for free flow from all oiling holes, then install plug and snap ring.

Lubricate camshaft and tappets generously during installation.

Lay each camshaft in place in its unloaded position, then install the bearing caps and tighten to the specified torque. Check cam end play.

Install the degree wheel and pointer and turn crankshaft to No. 1 TDC as described in Camshaft Timing.

Turn the crankshaft counterclockwise 45 degrees, then turn the right bank intake cam approximately 160 degrees counterclockwise until the timing mark on the cam gear flange is in alignment with the timing mark on No. 1 cam bearing cap.

Turn the crankshaft clockwise back to TDC, then install the cam gear (two bolts will hold the gear until all cam gears are installed).

Turn the crankshaft counterclockwise 45 degrees, then turn the left bank exhaust cam approximately 130 degrees clockwise until the timing mark on the cam gear flange is in alignment with the timing mark on No. 1 cam bearing cap.

Turn the crankshaft clockwise back to TDC, then install the cam gear.

Turn the right bank exhaust cam approximately 52 degrees counterclockwise until the timing mark on the cam gear flange is in alignment with the timing mark on the No. 1 cam bearing cap, then install the cam gear.

Turn the left bank intake cam approximately 20 degrees clockwise until the timing mark on the cam gear flange is in alignment with the timing mark on No. 1 cam bearing cap, then install the cam gear.

Check the valves for .100 lift at the specified crank angle as described in Camshaft Timing.

21

MAINTENANCE

Camshaft and Accessory Drive Gear Cover

Before installation of the cover, thoroughly clean in a degreasing solution and air-dry. Warm the cover to 150°–200°F to allow hand installation of the ball bearings. Lubricate the bearings with SAE 50 engine oil before installation.

Apply Hylomar Universal Jointing Compound to the cover mounting surfaces, then apply No. 50 silk thread as shown in Figure 30.

Position the cover, install the bolts and tighten to the specified torque in the sequence shown in Figure 50.

Check the gear backlash. If the backlash is not to specification, extra-lash gears are available. The method of using a dial indicator to check the backlash is shown in Figure 31.

Check the end play of the gears. If not to specifications, install spacers behind the bearings or grind the gear shoulders as required.

Check the distributor pilot in the gear cover. It must be concentric with the pitch diamater of the spline on the cam gear within .005 TIR. Also, the distributor mounting face must be square with the axis of the cam gear spline pitch diameter within .005 TIR.

The fuel pump pilot hole in the cover must be concentric with the camshaft bearing bore within .012 TIR, and square with the camshaft bearing bore within .005 TIR.

The tachometer pilot in the gear cover must be concentric to the tachometer drive slot within .006 TIR, and the mounting flange must be square with the axis of the slot within .008 TIR.

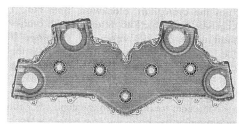

Figure 30 – Inside View of Gear Cover with Bearings Installed and Sealer and Silk Thread Applied

Figure 31 – Gear Train Backlash Check

Figure 32 – Method of Checking Distributor Pilot Concentricity

22

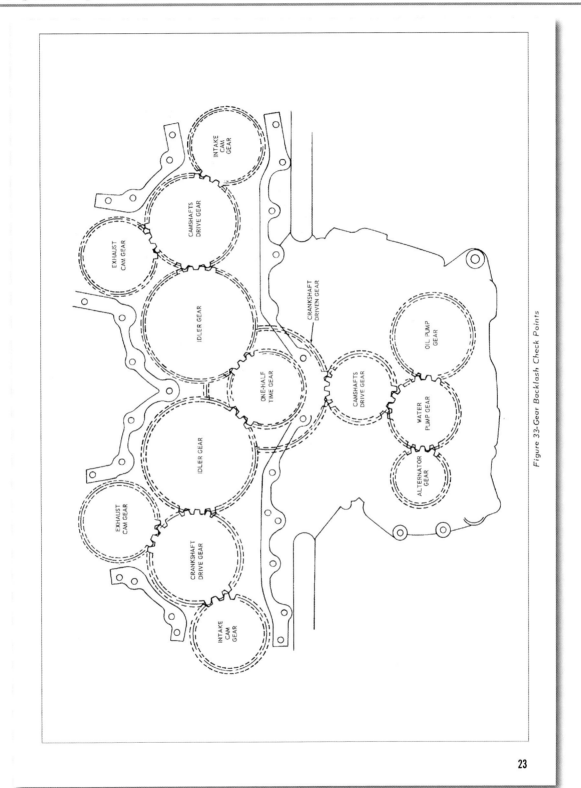

Figure 33-Gear Backlash Check Points

23

MAINTENANCE

Lubrication System

Oil Pumps

After the initial assembly ot the pressure and scavenage oil pumps they were flow-tested. The pressure pump produced a minimum of 3.0 gpm at 725-750 rpm, with 45 psi outlet pressure. The oil pressure relief valve opened at 85-90 psi at 728 rpm.

Both front and rear scavenge pumps produced a minimum of 2.5 gpm at 440-445 rpm with 45 psi outlet pressure.

The oil used in both tests was SAE 20 at 180° F.

When installing the complete oil pump assemblies, the interconnecting shafts must be in alignment for free rotation. Adjust the alignment by altering the tightening sequence of the cover bolts. Do not complete tightening or lockwire the oil pumps until the engine front cover is installed. The oil inlet and outlet tubes must be free to align with the engine front cover when it is positioned.

When installing the oil pump assemblies on the engine, install the front retaining nut first before the assembly is fully seated. This allows clearance between the top of the stud and the pump housing.

Use a wrench as shown in Figure 35 to tighten the nut to the specified torque.

When the oil filter is removed for cleaning, it must be handled carefully to avoid damage to the filter disc stack.

Backflush the filter disc stack in clean solvent to remove foreign particles, then airblow between discs. Direct the air flow in a tangential direction back and forth along disc stack. Caution – Do not use extreme pressure or attempt to disassemble the disc stack.

Immerse the filter in a final rinse of clean solvent, air dry, then assemble and install on engine.

Figure 34 - Install the oil Pump Forward Retaining Nut Before Pumps are Seated

Figure 35 - Special Wrench Used for Tightening Oil Pump Front Retaining Nut to Specified Torque.

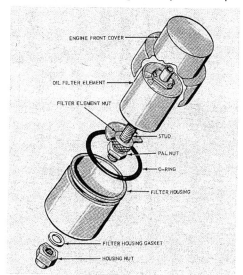

ENGINE FRONT COVER

OIL FILTER ELEMENT

FILTER ELEMENT NUT

STUD

PAL NUT

O-RING

FILTER HOUSING

FILTER HOUSING GASKET

HOUSING NUT

Figure 36 - Disassembled View of Oil Filter

24

MAINTENANCE

Pistons and Connecting Rods

Before installing the pistons and rods during engine overhaul, remove all deposits from the piston surfaces. Clean gum or varnish from the piston skirt, piston pins, and rings with solvent. Do not use a caustic cleaning solution or a wire brush to clean pistons.

To install the piston on the rod, install one spiral lock retainer in the piston bore, position the rod, install the piston pin, then install the second spiral retaining ring. Install the spiral retaining rings with the outer ends below the notch in the piston bore. This will facilitate future disassembly.

Production pistons are marked with a cone point on the piston head, and rods are marked with a forged button at the center side. When assembling the rod to the piston, the forged button should be upward and the cone point to the left of the button. When installing the connecting rod bearings, the bearing lock slots must be to the right of the forged button on the rod.

Check the ring gap in the cylinder, then install the rings on the piston. Position the rings on the piston as shown in Figure 38. Note that No. 1 compression ring has more tension and a wider gap in the free position. Be sure it is installed in the top ring groove.

Lubricate the cylinder bore before installing the piston and rod assemblies. Be sure the cone point on the piston head is to the outboard side of the engine, and the large chamfer of the connecting rod is toward the fillet of the crankshaft.

Figure 37 - Disassembled View of Piston and Connecting Rod

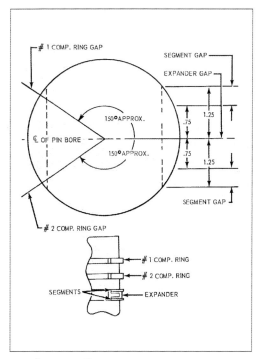

Figure 38 - Piston Ring Installation on Piston

25

MAINTENANCE

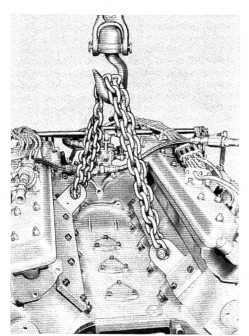

Figure 39 - After Removal of the Exhaust Manifolds, This Type of Lifting Sling May Be Used to Remove and Replace Engine.

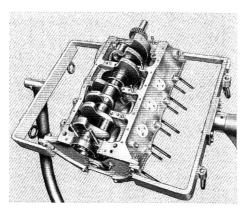

Figure 40 - Engine Holding Fixture As Used In Overhaul Stand

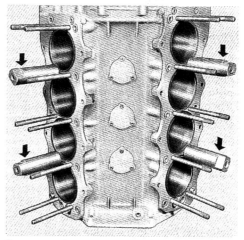

Figure 41 - Whenever the Cylinder Block is Immersed In Hot Degreaser, the Above Method Should Be Used to Retain the Liners In the Bloc.

Figure 42 - Cylinder Head-to-Block Seal Installation. Be Sure the Seal Is Installed With the Folded Outer Edge DOWN In the Head Deck of the Block.

26

MAINTENANCE

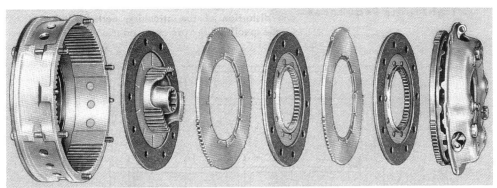

Figure 43 - Disassembled View of Clutch Assembly

The clutch assembly supplied with the Ford D.O.H.C. engine is the "Limited" model supplied by Borg and Beck of England. Service in the U.S.A. is currently being handled by Meyer-Drake, 2001 West Gage St., Los Angeles, California.

Clutch Maintenance

Do not use oil-base solvents for cleaning any part of the clutch.

Use alcohol to clean the metal parts of the clutch. Do not use alcohol on the clutch facings.

Clutch facings should be sanded lightly with a fine-grade sandpaper or emory cloth to decrease the glaze.

Use a minimum amount of lubricant on the clutch pilot or release bearing to prevent lubricant from entering the clutch.

Do not tighten clutch mounting bolts in excess of 12-14 ft lbs torque. Overtightening may cause failure of the clutch ring.

Particular attention should be given to the release bearing adapter (cross section shown in Figure 44) to provide a tight fit of the bearing in the adapter bore.

Lock tabs have been provided for the clutch assembly, and should be replaced each time the clutch is disassembled.

CLUTCH SPECIFICATIONS	
Borg and Beck Part Number	CP 2102
Ford Part Number	C5FE 7B546-A
Maximum Spin Speed	14,000 rpm
Weight	11 lbs 4 oz
Release Bearing Clearance	.100" Maximum
Release Travel	.250" Maximum
Overall Width (Including Cover)	2.250"
Input Spline Diameter	1-1/8"-10- Spline

The thrust on the release bearing to release the clutch is approximately 75 percent more than for an equivalent helical spring clutch, although the travel is less. Therefore, it is important that the travel allowance should not exceed .250 when selecting lever ratios.

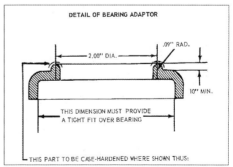

Figure 44 - Clutch Bearing Adapter

27

MAINTENANCE
Tightening Sequences

The tightening sequences shown must be used when assembling the engine to help prevent leaks and distortion of the attaching parts. Other torque specifications are given on page 5.

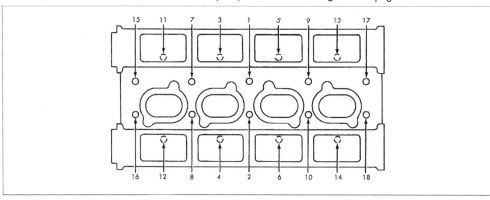

Figure 45 - Cylinder Head Tightening Sequence Torque is progressively increased in two steps.

1st step - Tighten Nos. 1,2,7,8,9,10,15,16, 17, and 18 to 30-40 ft-lbs torque.
- Tighten Nos. 3,4,5,6,11,12,13, and 14 hand tight.

2nd step - Tighten Nos. 1,2,7,8,9,10,15,16, 17, and 18 to 70-80 ft-lbs torque.
- Tighten Nos. 3,4,5,6,11,12,13, and 14 to 25-35 ft-lbs torque.

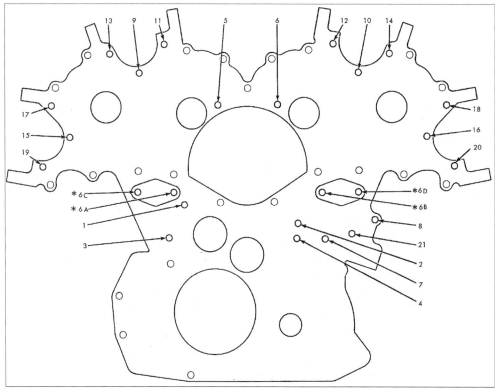

Figure 46 - Front Cover-to-Cylinder Block Tightening Sequence. Tighten Halfway in Sequence, then Repeat to Specified Torque.

28

(Tightening Sequences Continued)

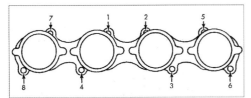

Figure 47 - Intake Manifold Tightening Sequence. Torque is progressively Increased in Two Steps.

1st step - Tighten to 8-10 ft-lbs Torque.
2nd step - Tighten to 12-15 ft-lbs Torque.

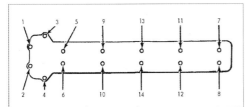

Figure 48 - Cam Tower Cover Tightening Sequence

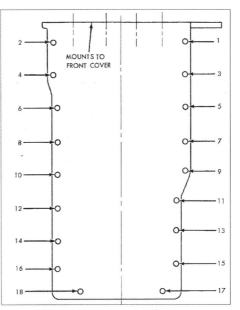

Figure 49 - Oil Pan-to-Cylinder Block Tightening Sequence.

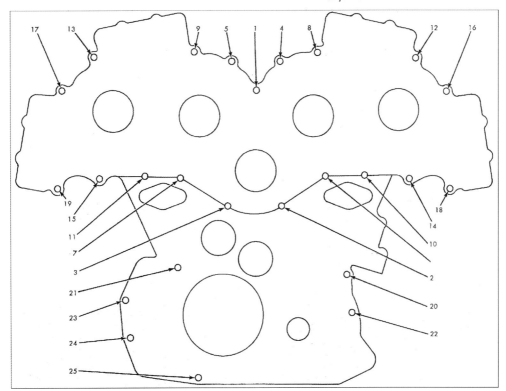

Figure 50 - Gear Cover and Front Cover Tightening Sequence. Tighten Halfway in Sequence, then Repeat to Specified Torque.

29

MAINTENANCE

Figure 51 - Safety Wiring Arrangement for Oil Pumps
and Rear Main Bearing Cap.

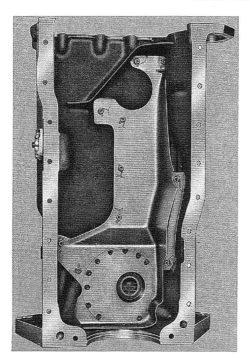

Figure 52 - Safety Wiring Arrangement for Oil Pan.
Baffle

Safety Wiring

Whenever safety wiring is removed it must
be replaced to help prevent loosening of attaching nuts and bolts. Use .032 diameter
stainless steel annealed safety wire, and install as shown in Figures 51 through 53.

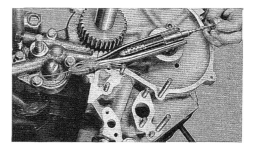

Figure 53 - Special Tool Used for Safety Wiring, Note
That Wire Must Be Turned To the Right,
In a Tightening Direction, Around the
Bolt Head.

30

MAINTENANCE

Exhaust System

Suitable tuning of the exhaust system can do much to improve engine performance. An exhaust system, based on the theroretical tube length of 71.6 was developed on the dynamometer. Then it was decided to pursue a one-half and one-quarter wave length study, since each of these offered advantages in accomodating the exhaust system to the vehicle. Accordingly, several systems were designed with various length tubes. Figure 54 shows a composite of the various systems tested. These ranged from single pipes to clusters which connected each head separately, all with optimum phasing.

The final selection for 1965 utilizes a one-half wave length pipe, with optimum phasing, and two divergent collector pipes. The lower right view of Figure 54 shows the final configuration. This system makes vehicle fuel calibration easier, and it is preferred by the majority of the drivers for the improvement in engine response after closed throttle.

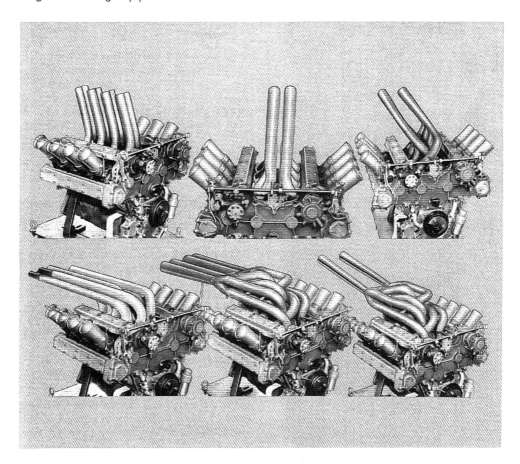

*Figure 54 - The Evolution of the Ford D.O.H.C.
Exhaust Configuration*

31

Chapter 8
Road racing the Ford 289ci Hi-Performance Engine

SPECIAL COMPONENTS & SPECIFICATIONS GROUP 2 SEDAN & GT40

While the Hi-Performance 289 engine had been very successful since introduction in March 1963, much effort was required to alter the cylinder heads for competition purposes, and the engines had proved fragile above 7000rpm in 1963-1965. Ford attempted to fix both aspects. In 1966 it released some special parts, such as a cylinder head kit, forged pistons, and stronger connecting rods, and for 1967 a four-bolt main cap block and a forged steel crankshaft. This was good for racers, who would likely win more races and keep Ford's name in the headlines, and for Ford's image as a maker of powerful and reliable engines.

The task of developing suitable high-performance parts was assigned to engineer Hank Lenox of Engine Engineering, in conjunction with Joe Eastman, Section Supervisor for high-performance engines, in 1965. Ford then released many all-out racing parts for the Hi-Performance 289ci engine in 1966 and 1967, sometimes referred to as 'E&F parts' because they were specially-made by the Engine and Foundry Division of the Ford Motor Company in Detroit. Ford listed these 289 parts as Special Components, Group 2 Sedan racing parts and GT-40 update parts, which were also often referred to as 'Heavy Duty' 289 parts.

Most of these special racing parts, and certainly any cast iron items, had

'FE' in the part number/casting coding. The 'F' meant 'non-production racing part' while the 'E' simply meant engine, as with all other Ford engines.

The 'Heavy Duty' road racing items were listed in Ford Dealership parts inventories, but were only available for distribution through Ford's designated racing parts master distributor Holman & Moody, situated on Wallace Neale Road in Charlotte, North Carolina. Any customer buying these parts would receive them from Holman & Moody, even if ordering from a Ford Main Dealer. Holman & Moody occupied a 175,000 square foot premises near the airport, and Ford's racing parts occupied about 10,000 square foot of it between 1965 and 1971 – an inventory worth $7,000,000.

The special cylinder head kit was a very significant introduction in 1966. It was available under part number S7MR-6049-A or as individual cylinder heads with part number C6FE-6049-A. The combustion chamber of these cylinder heads was similar in shape to the original 221ci and the 1963 model year 289ci-2V engine components, only it was larger than both to accommodate its larger inlet and exhaust valves with maximum possible clearance between the perimeter edges of the valves and the combustion chamber walls. Inlet valve head diameter was 1.875in, it had a 30 degree inlet valve seat for increased flow capability, and the exhaust valves had a head diameter of 1.625in with a conventional 45 degree valve seat. Single valve springs with a flat wound damper were used. The inlet and exhaust ports were larger as cast than on any previous cast iron small block. The valves were un-shrouded as much as possible, which resulted in a 63.5cc chamber volume, requiring the use of raised-top pistons to raise compression to 10.5:1 when used in conjunction with new Ford steel shim head gaskets. These racing cylinder heads were excellent bolt-on items. Each had a casting code of C6FE-6090-A on the exterior, in between two exhaust ports, and some had 'R.J.' by the pushrod slots, adjacent to the second and third rocker arms in from the end of the head, which refers to a special heat treatment code. These cylinder heads were all made on the 'jobbing floor' of the Dearborn Iron Foundry. The jobbing floor was separate from the main production line and where low volume or special parts were made.

The new 1966 C6FE-6015-A block was a strengthened version of the original stock production block. It was made from the same Ford grade AC cast iron material, but had thicker wall sections and physically larger nodular iron main caps than those of the Hi-performance 289. The main caps were made from a stronger 80% nodular iron material, as opposed to Ford's ACB grade of cast iron.

Steel shim, right-hand (C6FE-6051-B) and left-hand (C6FE-6083-B) bank fitting head gaskets 0.032in thick were developed by Ford to increase compression ratio. Other new parts for 1966 included four-into-one tubular exhaust manifolds that fitted a Mustang.

The Ford 289ci GT-40 update crankshafts available from mid-1967 were forged steel, had cross-drilled oil ways, and were counterweighted differently from stock cast iron items for reduced bearing loading. These particular crankshafts are easy to recognise via their marked, as forged, C7FE6303B code. Besides being used to update a GT-40 engine, these crankshafts were, of course, able to fit into a stock Hi-Performance 289 block used in sedan racing, such as the Mustang, while retaining the use of the original Hi-Performance 289ci engine block, supplementary counterweight, flywheel, and crankshaft damper.

The 1966 'Heavy Duty' connecting rods had different raw forgings to the Hi-Performance 289ci items, and were made from a higher grade of high tensile steel. The bolt head machining was not broached, like production Hi-Performance items, but 'spot faced' to take the 'football'-shaped heads of the connecting rod bolts. This was the second time that Ford engineers increased connecting rod strength in this specific area by removing a minimum of material from the forging in the bolt head area. The first instance was the all-alloy 255ci pushrod engine used at Indianapolis 500 in 1963. These connecting rods were fatigue-tested to 7000rpm, and were more durable than the stock broached Hi-Performance 289ci components.

The 1967 GT-40 update, casting coded XE-136136 cylinder block was much the same as the previous year's C6FE-6015-A item upon which it was based. However, the 1967 edition had further strengthening and featured 80% nodular iron material four-bolt main caps on the centre three main bearings.

FORD BOOKLET

The information that follows is an extract from the Ford booklet illustrated below. It lists the entire range of special components.

Introduction

This booklet is designed for owners of Ford's Hi-Performance 289ci engine, especially those who utilize this version of the 289 for road racing circuits and are interested in obtaining even greater performance and durability. The introduction of new performance components, specifications, and installation tolerances contained herein are written for experienced personnel,

Figure 1. Hi-Performance 289ci V8 engine.

The eight cylinder Hi-Performance 289 CID engine puts out 0.95 horsepower per cubic inch, and weighs only two pounds per horsepower. The bore is an even four inches, and the stroke is 2.870 inches. The very high bore-to-stroke ratio provides other advantages which include low piston speed, reduced frictional losses, and the use of large overhead valves to promote good breathing characteristics.

The torque peak is 312lb-ft at 3400rpm. Compression ratio is 10.5:1, and the engine is fed by a four-venturi carburettor.

Preparing the Hi-Performance 289 CID for sedan racing
Special exhaust headers – part number S1MR-9428-B

The kit includes 289 sedan exhaust headers specially tuned to provide maximum efficiency and reduce back pressure.

Performance improvement
Provides increased horsepower and

and not intended as a step-by-step instruction guide. All parts contained in this booklet may be obtained from Shelby American.

Since its development in 1963, Ford's 289ci V8 engine has become one of the most popular competition engines to enter the world of racing.

There are three versions of Ford's basic 289ci engine: the 200 horsepower; the 225 horsepower, and the 271 horsepower. The 271 horsepower Hi-Performance version differs from the lower two economy engines by having beefier rods, hotter cam, special four-barrel carburettor, solid lifters, high efficiency exhaust headers, etc. This engine is used as the basic power for the Shelby Mustang GT-350, Ford GT-40 and many other race cars.

The new racing engine components mentioned on the

following pages are designed to update the 271 horsepower version of the 289ci engine.

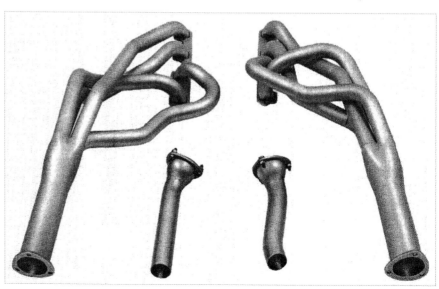

Figure 2. 289 sedan exhaust header kit.

imparts improved performance at high rpm levels.

Special camshaft kit – part number S7MR-6250-A

This kit includes the camshaft and 16 pushrods to be used with the regular production high-performance tappets of the 271 horsepower engine under part number S7MR-6250-A.

Performance improvement

The camshaft provides superior breathing, due to increased cam duration revised timing and higher valve toss speed. It increases output to 6800rpm with a toss speed of approximately 7500rpm when used in conjunction with cylinder head kit C7MR-6049-A. This camshaft kit is especially suited to road racing.

Camshaft lift is 0.507in, intake lash is 0.020in, exhaust lash is 0.025in, inlet duration 318 degrees, exhaust duration 304 degrees, overlap is 94 degrees, valve spring seated pressure is 85-95lb at a 1.820in fitted height, and fully open pressure is 270-280lb.

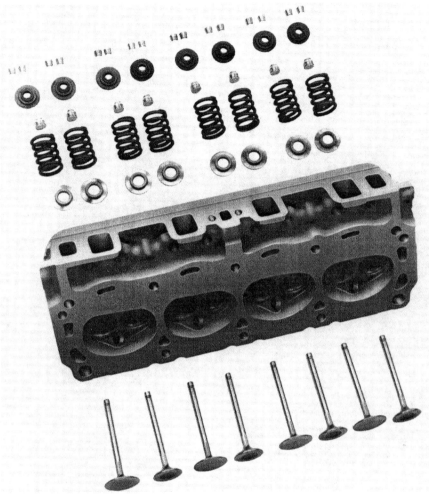

Figure 4. Cylinder head assembly kit.

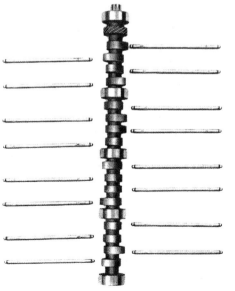

Figure 3. Camshaft kit.

Special cylinder head kit – part number S7MR-6049-A

The kit includes fully modified 289 CID cylinder heads for sedan racing needs; larger 1.875in intake and 1.625in exhaust valves. Springs, retainers, teflon valve stem seals, etc, are furnished. Cylinder heads should be used with the specified steel shim head gaskets shown in the parts list.

Performance improvement

Output increases when used in conjunction with the high-performance camshaft and induction system. This power increase is accomplished through improved porting, revised combustion chamber, and increased valve size. Individual cylinder head part number C6FE-6049-A.

Special induction kit – part number C6ZZ-6B068-A

This kit contains two 4-venturi Holley carburettors on a cast aluminium high-riser inlet manifold. Also included is an air cleaner assembly, progressive linkage, and gaskets.

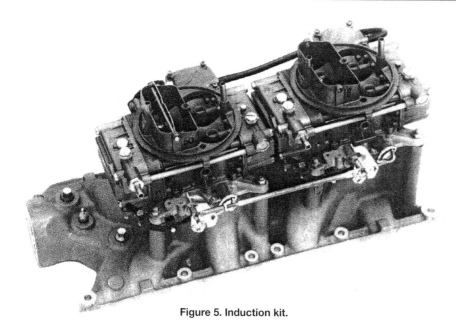

Figure 5. Induction kit.

Performance improvement

Increases output at maximum rpm; progressive linkage affords smooth operation throughout the entire rpm range. Large ports and long runners plus half-moon floats create excellent results for road racing.

Special piston kit – part number S7MR-6109-A

Kit includes eight racing pistons, eight piston pins, eight connecting rods, rings and bearings. This kit should be used with cylinder head kit C7MR-6049-A. Use C5OE-6211-H or J or C6FE-6221-A connecting rod bearings in conjunction with the above piston and rod assembly kit. Choose bearings to insure proper selective fit. The

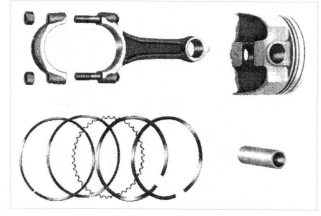

Figure 6. Piston and rod assembly kit.

present high-performance crankshaft must be rebalanced with a 760 gram bob-weight when using this kit.

Performance improvement

Each piston is fabricated from extruded aluminium and cam ground. Connecting rods are fatigue-tested at 7000rpm. These pistons when used with the S7MR-6049-A cylinder heads, which have larger combustion chambers than the production 289 Hi-Performance engine, provide a compression ratio of 10.5:1.

Assembly specifications of interest

• Main bearing clearances 0.002-0.0025in
• Big end clearances 0.002-0.0025in
• Crankshaft end play 0.004in-0.008in
• Side clearance of two connecting rod big ends on each crank-pin 0.022-0.032in
• Piston to bore clearance 0.005-0.006in
• Crankshaft damper to crankshaft snout must have 0.001in interference fit
• Cylinder head torque 70-80ft-lb: 20 ft-lb first step and 10ft-lb increments from then on

Special 289ci component part numbers for sedan racing

• Cylinder head kit S7MR-6049-A
• Cylinder head assembly C6FE-6049-A
• 1.625in exhaust valve C6FE –6505-A
• 1.875in inlet valve C6FE-6507-A
• Valve springs C2AE-6A511-C
• Valve spring retainer C6FE-6514-A
• Valve spring seat C7FE-6A536-A
• Split locks 7HA-6518-A1
• Valve stem seals C5FE-6A517-B
• Head gasket: left-hand C6FE-6083-B
• Head gasket: right-hand C6FE 6051-B
• Piston and connecting rod assembly kit S7MR-6109-A
• Piston and connecting rod assembly C7FE-6100-A
• Piston C6FE-6110-A
• Top compression ring C6FE-6150-A
• Second compression ring C6FE-6152-A
• Oil control ring CC6FE-6159-A & C6FE-6161-A
• Connecting rod C6FE-6200-A
• Piston pin C7FE-6135-A
• Camshaft kit S7MR-6250-A
• Camshaft C7FE-6250-A
• Pushrods C6FE-6565-A
• High pressure oil pump C6FE-6600-A

Updating the GT-40 OHV 289 CID V-8 engine

This section is written specifically for owners of the 289ci GT-40 engine, particularly those interested in updating their current engine.

The standard engine in your Ford GT-40 is a 289ci 90 degree V-8. The original version of this powerplant developed 375bhp at 6800rpm. The bore and stroke are 4.000x2.870in, and the compression ratio is 10.5:1.

The components listed on the following pages are designed primarily to update the engine for increased durability and performance. The new engine block provides beefed-up main bearing webs and pan rails. It also incorporates four-bolt main caps in the centre three positions for improved durability.

Figure 9. The camshaft is the same as the 1966 Le Mans one, except it's a new casting to insure uniform lobe hardness and machining.

Figure 10. The new crankshaft has revised counterweights to reduce the main bearing loads.

Figure 11. The new piston pin is a cantilevered design for greater fatigue life.

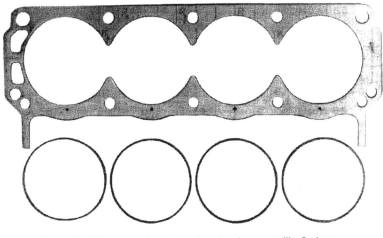

Figure 12. This new cylinder head gasket has metallic O-rings with a periphery mattress.

Figure 7. New 4-bolt block.

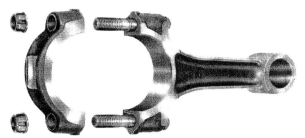

Figure 8. The new connecting rod assembly has been fatigue-tested at 7000rpm.

Torque specifications

- Main cap 7/16in bolts x ten: 75-85ft-lb
- Main cap bolts x six: 35-40ft-lb
- Connecting rod bolt nuts: 45-50ft-lb
- Damper fit on crankshaft: 0.001in interference fit

1967 GT-40 update component part numbers

- Cylinder block C7FE-6010-A
- Cylinder heads C6FE-6049-A
- Piston C7FE-6110-B
- Piston pin C7FE-6135-A
- Connecting rod C7FE-6200-A
- Camshaft C7FE-6250-A
- Valve springs C7FE-6A536-A
- Forged steel crankshaft C7FE6303B

Chapter 9

'Tunnel Port' 302ci racing engines of 1968

The 'Tunnel Port' technology had worked so well on the 427ci FE big block engines in NASCAR racing that Ford Division decided to apply it to the small block engine for use in Mustangs.

These engines were all made under code RX-395, and approximately 210 were built. This all took place in the days when Ford management was keen on big inlet ports and maximum possible air flow, and would not be swayed away from this criteria by Ford Engine engineers who warned of the potential problems that could occur. The plan was to provide these racing engines to Mustang racing teams, and also offer a Dealer Service Option engine conversion kit for road use to private Mustang owners. The kit would include cylinder heads, inlet manifold, carburettor, and exhaust manifolds and be available to buy over the counter at Ford Dealers with the option of fitting.

The Tunnel Port racing engine programme was a Ford Division initiative; that is, it was financed by the Ford Division that built the Mustang. The programme was a cylinder head and inlet manifold development based on the earlier 289 'Heavy Duty'/Group 2/ GT-40 update short assembly hardware – such as block, crankshaft, connecting rods and pistons – but with a 3in stroke crankshaft to fit the 302ci engine size. Design and development happened in 1967 and the early part of 1968, under the direction of Hank Lenox of Engine Engineering, in conjunction with Joe Eastman, Section Supervisor for high-performance engines. A large number of support draughtsmen, mechanics and dynamometer operators were also involved, and the programme lasted about 18 months.

Approximately 70 racing engines were made in the EEE build shop for a number of racing teams. However, the racing engines were not successful in SCCA Trans-Am racing. They were found to lack the mid-range torque vital for off the turns and out of corners in circuit racing. This resulted in drivers turning the engines higher than the recommended 7000-7500rpm (up to 8000-8500rpm), causing the 'bottom ends' to fail. The inlet ports were simply far too large, in fact they were nearly as large as those of the 427ci FE Tunnel Port engines. This, coupled with the turbulence caused by the pressed-in steel tube situated in the middle of the port, meant that the engines lacked good air flow.

The top-end power was never in doubt though, with 500bhp available at 7000rpm. This was the maximum rpm that Ford recommended, and the engines were, by-and-large, very reliable at this speed due to the specialised racing components fitted. These characteristics actually made the engines very appropriate for drag racing, and many were used for this purpose.

The planned production dealer installed kits were never made (except for a few development engine kits), due to the disappointing performance of the racing engines. They would have had smaller valves and ball pivot rocker arms, much the same as a stock 302ci engine, which was quite a different arrangement to the 70 racing versions that had rocker shafts with forged adjustable rocker arms.

All Tunnel Port racing engines used a strengthened block that had four-bolt main caps on the centre three mains. This block was essentially the GT-40 289ci update component released in 1967, but now with screw-in freeze plugs, as opposed to press-in. The block casting code was C8FE-6015B.

These racing engines all used the Cooper mechanical joint O-ring cylinder bore to cylinder head sealing system in conjunction with the 'dry-deck' block to cylinder head arrangement, as per the 1963 Indianapolis 500 pushrod V8 engines with neoprene 'O'-rings to seal the coolant transfer between the block and cylinder head. With individual cylinder bore and cylinder head sealing, and the absence of coolant sealing via a conventional type head gasket, if a cylinder's sealing became compromised combustion would leak harmlessly into the atmosphere, rather than passing into the cooling system, pressurising it, and causing engine failure. The draw-back of this system was the exacting and expensive machining of the engine components necessary to accept the Cooper mechanical joint and neoprene O-rings.

Ford engineers decided to use the original head gasket system of the Indianapolis 500 255ci V8 engine with Cooper mechanical joint O-rings, but sized to suit the 4in bore because of the head gasket issues experienced in recent years at Le Mans.

The crankshaft was forged steel with a 3in stroke. It was also counterweighted for reduced bearing loads; the third counterweights in from each end of the crankshaft were phased 90 degrees to the first and second ones, and 180 degrees apart from each other, as per the first revision on the Hi-Performance 289ci forged steel item in mid-1967 designed to reduce the bearing loading. The big end journals were cross-drilled for improved oiling. The crankshaft was also fitted with the Hi-Performance 289ci engine's 5.9oz-in external balance supplementary counterweight, camshaft sprocket, and timing chain arrangement. As with the Hi-Performance 289, this was to reduce the external counterweighting positioned on the hub of the crankshaft damper. The counterweighting is moved closer to the front main bearing to reduce the bending moment of the crankshaft at high rpm that occurs due to the external balance mass being well forward on the front of the crankshaft. The amount of external balance front and rear was reduced to approximately 15oz-in in total, with the approximate 9.0oz-in of external balance being carried on the hub of the new C8FE-6316-B crankshaft damper designed by Simpson Industries specifically for the 302ci Tunnel Port racing engine.

The road-going Tunnel Port engines were to use a stock length 5.090in centre-to-centre distance heavy-duty forged connecting rod with part number C8FE-6200-A. This was stronger than the stock 302ci item and provided a 1.69:1 connecting rod to stroke ratio. The Tunnel Port racing engines, on the other hand, used the 1964-65 Indianapolis 500 connecting rods. These had a 5.316in centre-to-centre distance, which, coupled with the 3in stroke, gave the engine a 1.77:1 connecting rod to stroke ratio.

During the time that Mustangs were being tested with Tunnel Port 302ci engines, Ford experimented with these engines equipped with earlier Heavy Duty 289ci GT-40 cylinder heads, as available from 1966. This increased the mid-range power, making it adequate, but reduced the top-end power to 450bhp at 7000rpm, which was regarded as insufficient. Ford Division stopped using Tunnel Port engines when it became apparent that these performed unsatisfactorily in circuit racing applications.

SPECIFIC TUNNEL PORT ENGINE COMPONENT PART NUMBERS

- Block: C8FE-6010B
- Forged steel crankshaft (3in stroke): C8FE-6300-A
- Crankshaft damper: C8FE-6316-B
- Flywheel: C8FE-6375-B
- Connecting rod: C8FE-6200-A
- Cylinder head: C8FE-6049-A

The C8FE-6316-B crankshaft damper, as designed and supplied by Simpson Industries, was also used with great success on the Boss 302 Trans-Am engines of 1969 and 1970, as well as 366ci Cleveland Nascar, and 351ci Cleveland drag racing engines of 1970s. This damper was regarded as excellent by Ford engineers; it minimised a valve train harmonic that generated a large dip on the torque curve of these engines, and no crankshafts failed during testing with these dampers. As this damper began to be used in Nascar by Bud Moore Engineering, and then the Woods Brothers, all available used Boss 302ci Trans-Am dampers were collected by Ford and sent to these two concerns for use on Nascar engines. More dampers of this type were produced and supplied on request to these two companies by Simpson Industries. This same basic damper was available from SVO in later years under part number M-6316-A3.

Chapter 10
Trans-Am Boss 302ci racing engines 1969-1970

The Boss 302ci racing engine was introduced in 1969 following the failure of the 302ci Tunnel Port racing engine in USA's 1968 SCCA Trans-Am Championship. The Engine and Foundry Division of the Ford Motor Company was asked by Ford Division to design a small block engine to replace the 1968 Tunnel Port 302ci in Mustangs for Trans-Am road racing.

At the time, in early 1968, development of the big port 4V 351ci Cleveland engine was progressing well, but wasn't yet complete, and Ford engineers decided to fit the cylinder heads from this engine to the existing small 302ci Tunnel Port racing engine blocks (it's generally accepted that this was Bill Gay's idea). The Cleveland engine and the 302ci small block engine both shared the same bore spacing (4.380in/111.2mm) and cylinder head bolt placement, and both had been designed to be produced on the same machine tooling in the Cleveland

Engine Plant, so the conversion was straightforward. Engineers modified existing Cleveland prototype cylinder heads for a different water flow path into the inlet manifold, to suit the 302ci small block arrangement, and when this proved to be successful, they modified Cleveland casting patterns to make what we know today as Boss 302ci engine cylinder heads. While being very similar to production Cleveland cylinder head castings, these were in fact a little different, but the end result was that Cleveland cylinder head technology was released on the Boss 302ci engine before the Cleveland engine was introduced.

The 351ci Cleveland engine had splayed pushrods and canted inlet and exhaust valves. The splaying of the pushrods was purely to accommodate larger inlet ports that weren't possible with parallel placed pushrods. This feature led to the canted inlet and exhaust valves, regarded by Ford

engine engineers as the best possible within the confines of a two valve pushrod-type V8 engine.

The flow capability of the Cleveland cylinder heads was well known to Ford engine engineers by this stage, and it seemed logical to fit them to the smaller engines for racing purposes. It was all done quite quickly, and it worked.

The Boss 302ci engines went into production in the Cleveland Engine Plant in July 1968 destined for 1969 Boss 302 Mustangs to be released in October 1968. To comply with Trans-Am racing homologation rules, Ford had to plan to produce at least 5000 Boss 302 Mustangs. Production of the Boss 302ci engine continued until the end of 1970, totalling more than 8600 units; the official figures being 1628 for 1969, and 7013 for 1970. This engine was also fitted into approximately 450 Mercury Cougar Eliminators.

A Boss 302 Mustang was placed second in the 1969 SCCA Trans-Am

Championship and first in 1970 using specially-made 'all-out' racing versions of the basic stock Boss 302ci engine. The construction of these particular engines was instigated by Bill Innes, Executive Vice President of the Ford Motor Company. His directive was to build racing engines that would allow the Mustangs to win the Trans-Am championship. The work was carried out in the EEE building by the Race Group of Avanced Engines under project manager Joe Macura, in conjunction with a staff of 41 engineers that were assigned to him by Bill Gay, chief engineer of the Engine and Foundry Division. These particular engines, a reported 115 of them, were quite different from the stock production Boss 302s. Anyone who believes the stock production Boss 302ci engines were converted into these racing engines needs to think again. The racing engines were very special factory-built versions available only to Ford-backed racers. The Trans-Am blocks, for example, were slightly different again from the 1968 Tunnel Port Trans-Am versions. Some of the earlier blocks had cracked in racing service, so these were made with thicker bore walls on the thrust face as well as the decks. The crankshaft essentially remained the same as the Tunnel Port items, but was made from a slightly higher specification material, while the C8FE Tunnel Port crankshaft damper, designed and made by Simpson Industries, was carried over to the Boss 302ci. The incredibly strong 1969-70 Trans-Am connecting rods (C9ZE-D) were very similar to the 1964-65 DOHC Indianaplis 500 and 1967-68 GT-40 Le Mans engine items. A centre-to-centre distance of 5.316in coupled with the 3in stroke gave the engine a 1.77:1 connecting rod to stroke ratio, and

the amount of external balance was reduced to 14.7oz-in front and rear. New forged pistons with a different crown shape than previous Tunnel Port technology engine items were made to suit the shape of the Cleveland cylinder head combustion chamber.

The 1969-1970 blocks and cylinder heads were machined for 'dry-decking' with Cooper mechanical joint O-ring cylinder bore sealing and neoprene rubber O-ring coolant transfer sealing, the same as the 1968 Tunnel Port racing engines. Each cylinder head now had an outlet at the front that piped the coolant via a bifurcated joint casting to the top of the radiator, as opposed to the coolant transferring from each cylinder head into the inlet manifold and then being piped to the top of the radiator. The dry-decking head gasket system was used in this very arduous, uncompromising environment because of the maximum reliability it more or less guaranteed. If a Cooper mechanical joint failed, for example, only that cylinder was affected. The combustion gases would vent into the atmosphere and not into the cooling system, causing the engine to fail due to it being pressurised.

The wet sump arrangement used a $\frac{3}{8}$in hexagon drive the same as the 351ci Windsor V8 engine (as opposed to the usual $\frac{5}{16}$in item), and the rear of the oil pan was scavenged by an extra pump positioned under, but integral to, the usual main pressure pump that drove it. This prevented oil from building up at the back of the pan, ensuring that the main oil pump pickup always had oil around it to draw in.

There was a succession of engine failures in 1969 that were initially of unknown origin, but later thought to be the fault of the engine bearings. When the bearing shells were returned to TRW for fault analysis, the journal facing

surfaces were put under a microscope and the findings reported back to Ford. On each occasion, it was reported that there appeared to be glass particulate matter embedded in the surface. It was not realised how this could be possible until the manufacturing processes of the engine components were backtracked. It was found that the fabricated aluminium sumps had been glass bead cleaned after welding, and in spite of thorough washing after this process, particles remained and kept being released into the oil, and therefore the oiling system. So the welder had glass bead cleaned the sumps after welding to make the job look good, but in doing so had unwittingly introduced a serious problem. Strict instructions were then issued that there was to be no more glass bead cleaning of sump welds. Existing sumps were rigorously inspected and all traces of glass bead ground-off before each sump was passed and able to be reused. There were no further issues of this type in 1969 or 1970.

1969 BOSS 302 RACING ENGINES

These engines featured exceptionally large inlet and exhaust valves and port cylinder heads, with twin four-barrel 4500 Holley carburettors a top a Ford engineer Denny Wu-designed individual runner inlet manifold. On average they developed a maximum of 360lb-ft of torque between 6400-6800rpm. This was a very narrow band; realistically too narrow for circuit racing. Maximum power of 505-510bhp was delivered at 7400-7500rpm, and the maximum permissible engine speed was 8200-8400rpm. These engines produced good top-end power, but the very narrow rpm band where high torque was available made them similar to, although better than the 1968 Tunnel Port. The cylinder heads used were either stock Boss 302ci or 351ci Cleveland 4V hydraulic camshaft engine items converted to suit a mechanical camshaft via pushrod guide plates and screw-in rocker studs. While many camshafts were tried, Ford engineers finally settled on their AA grind, although this was replaced later in the year with their E2 which was used exclusively throughout 1970. The stock road-going engine Boss 302ci Morse chain and sprockets were used both years. The final four-into-one exhaust system configuration used 2¼in diameter primary pipes approximately 40in long, quadruplicating into a 4in main pipe that was flattened off for ground clearance and side exiting.

1970 BOSS 302 RACING ENGINES

On average these engines developed a maximum of 365lb-ft of torque at 6000rpm, 360lb-ft at 5500rpm and 6500rpm, dropping to 350lb-ft at 7000rpm. Maximum power of 475bhp was delivered at 7400-7500rpm, and maximum permissible engine speed was 8200-8400rpm. The 1970 engine was better for road racing than its 1969 predecessor, even though it had less maximum power, because the same amount of torque was spread over a much wider rpm band. This was due in the main to Ford Engineer Denny Wu spending a lot of time developing new, smaller inlet ports and reducing valve sizes for the cylinder heads that Ford made specially for these racing engines this year, as well as a major inlet manifold that resulted in the 'Mini Plenum' 4V. With these all-new, racing-only cylinder heads in conjunction with a new inlet manifold and single 850CFM four-barrel 4150 Holley carburettor, these engines were, without a doubt, at least equal to anything else in Trans-Am, if not slightly better. Combine all of this with Bud Moore Engineering car preparation and Parnelli Jones' driving ability, and the result was bound to be good.

Chapter 11
Boss 302 Engine Modifications for Strip and Track – 1970 catalogue

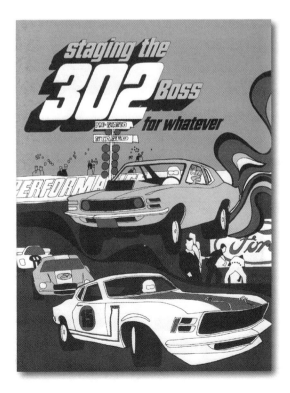

street 'n strip

The 302 BOSS may be the best regular production Ford engine ever. Certainly it rates tops among small blockers. The only comparable mill to date is the 427. Like 427 engines, the BOSS 302 comes from the factory with many high performance components as shown on page 6. Their design and durability is superior to regular production engines for applications ranging from normal "street" use up to most "stock" classes at the strip. For that reason, "Staged" Muscle Parts kits are not required for 302 BOSS engines. However, these "Staged-Tuning" tricks increase response and add a significant horsepower increase as explained on pages 7-9.

stage-tuning the 302 Boss

 **induction**

Carburetor . . . . Install larger jets
Install weaker diaphragm spring
Intake Manifold . . . Block heat riser passage
Fuel Pump . . . . Install electric unit at fuel tank
Thermactor . . . . Remove belt or complete system

 **ignition timing**

Distributor . . . . Remove or disconnect "Limiter"
Remove dual advance distributor and install dual breaker point kit, or complete 289HP dual point distributor.
Spark Plugs . . . . . Install colder plugs
Wiring . . . . Install "steel core" for strip only

 **exhaust headers**

Exhaust Manifold . . . Replace with steel tube "headers"

 **modified heads**

Heads . . . . Port and polish cylinder heads

 **chassis tips**

Transmission . . . . . Modify blocker rings
Rear Axle . . . . Use high ratio ring and pinion gears, and "No-Spin" Detroit Locker differential
Suspension . . . . . . Install traction bars, spring clamps and pinion bumper

competition only

for serious racers... a special book

That's right. For you guys who want to build a highly modified drag-ster . . . make a big left turn in NASCAR GT . . . or run with Parnelli Jones in Trans Am machines. Obviously, that scene requires a super-trick engine. Which you can build with super trick "Competition Only" Muscle Parts. We gave them a unique name because they're designed specifically for strip 'n track competition. You order them just like any other Muscle Part. But remember. Competition Only parts are specially designed and manufactured low volume pieces . . . ,making them more expensive than the "streetable" types of Muscle Parts.

But Ford figures if you'd like to make it your thing, the least we could do is tell you how. Can you dig it?

We think you will because there's a bin-full of "Competition Only" pieces available for the first time. Things like unbelievably beefy con rods, special bearings, roller bearing rocker arms, Titanium valves, in-line intake manifold and matching carburetors. Ford performance engineers take you through detailed engine blueprinting procedures . . . including how to port and polish the heads. And much more as you can see from the Table of Contents.

table of contents

to get a copy

Enclose:
$2.00 per copy (check or money order)

Ask For:
"BOSS 302 Engine Modification for Strip/Track" Form MP 1069.

Also available
302 Boss Chassis Modifications
Form MP 1070
Price $2.00

Address request to:

Muscle Parts Headquarters P.O. Box 5386
Milwaukee Junction Station Detroit, Michigan 48211

302 Boss engine

302 BOSS is more than just a name. It's a statement of fact. No other small block engine has ever come from the factory with a greater array of high revving pieces. They plain flat out make it . . . the all-time BOSS. Here's a look at some of the high performance parts that come as standard equipment on 302 BOSS engines.

production 302 Boss specifications

Nominal (inches) except as shown

Displacement (Cu. In.)	302
Carburetor	4V, 780 CFM
Horsepower (Bhp @ rpm)	290 @ 5800
Torque (Lb. Ft. @ rpm)	290 @ 4300
Compression Ratio	10.5:1
Bore	4.00
Stroke	3.00
Bore Spacing	4.38
Head Volume (c.c.)	61.3–64.3 (69) 57.0–60.0 (70)
Crankshaft -- Material -- Journal Dia -- Main -- Rod	Forged Steel 2.2486 2.1226
Con Rods -- Material -- Length (Ctr. - Ctr.)	Forged Steel 5.150
Pistons -- Material -- Compression Height -- Deck Clearance	Forged Aluminum 1.529 0.013 - 0.033
Centerline of Crank to top of Block	8.201 - 8.211
Camshaft -- Timing -- Open/Close -- Duration/Overlap Lift -- Journal Dia.	Int - 34°/76° Exh - 86°/24° 290°/58° 0.290'' No. 1—2.081 No. 2—2.066 No. 3—2.051 No. 4—2.036 No. 5—2.021
Tappets	Mechanical
Rocker Arm -- Ratio -- Type	1.73:1 Lightweight stamping with Threaded Stud-Adj.
Valves -- Head Dia -- Intake -- Exhaust	2.225 - 2.235 (69) 2.185 - 2.195 (70) 1.702 - 1.717
Valve Stem Diameter	0.342''
Valve Spring Load - Closed (Lbs. @ Installed Ht) - Open	88-96 @ 1.82 299-331 @ 1.32
Firing Order	1-5-4-2-6-3-7-8
Initial Advance (Vacuum Disconnected)	16° BTDC
Breaker Point - Gap - Dwell	0.020 30° - 33°
Spark Plug Gap	0.032 - 0.036
Manifold Vacuum (Idle)	11 inches of mercury

block

Beefy lower end webbing and heavy 4-bolt main bearing caps at No. 2, 3 and 4 journals resist cap flexing, which maintains more precise alignment even in the ultra high 6000 to 8500 rpm range. Number 1 and 5 journals use conventional 2-bolt caps. The oil pan baffle covers the caps. It keeps the crank from excessively splashing oil around during high rpm operation, which lessens oil frothing and aeration.

NOTE: For all-out competition, use a deep sump oil pan.

crankshaft

Machined from forged steel that has greater strength and rigidity than conventional iron crank. Can be used with all modifications including injection and super-charging.

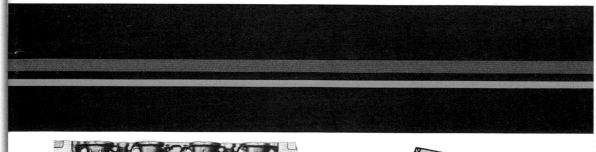

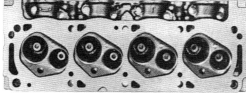

combustion chamber

Basic design is partial quench wedge. However, canting the valves produces an arc-shaped chamber top . . . giving it a touch of hemi. This permits large valve head diameters and less shrouding to improve breathing. Page 15 illustrates 351 Cleveland canted valve angularity . . . which is identical to 302 BOSS. Because of the many angles, "polyangle wedge" is often used to describe this combustion chamber.

heads

Huge (2.50" x 1.75") rounded intake ports promote highly efficient airflow and breathing capabilities. Note "canted" (angled) non-parallel valve stems.

cam and valve train

Solid tappet mechanical cam, stamped lightweight rocker arms, "sled" fulcrums, threaded studs, hardened push rods and guide plates minimize "play" in the valve train to keep everything in shape during high revs.

rods and pistons

Sturdy forged steel rods operate safely on drag strip during brief 7000 rpm revs . . . or as high as 7500 when polished and "shot-peened". For sustained operation over 7500 rpm, use "Competition Only" rods. Instead of the conventional cast pistons with the pin offset to reduce piston slap, 302 BOSS pistons are forged for greater strength.

induction

The biggest flowing carburetor Ford offers on a production engine . . . a 4V 780 CFM Holley, sits atop a lightweight aluminum intake manifold with high rise runners to promote free breathing through it's big rounded ports.

stage tuning the 302 BOSS

The 302 BOSS likes to rev. The higher the better. As rpm increases, its breathing capabilities rise at a rapid rate . . . so it's very sensitive to modifications in this area. In factory trim, the dual advance distributor and "closed" exhaust system adversely affect performance above 5000 rpm. Around 6150 rpm the distributor limiter actually causes the engine to "cut-out" or miss by interrupting the spark. Similarly, relatively lean carburetion and retarded spark due to emission control specifications, sap performance.

Enriched carburetion and advanced ignition timing improves performance and actually results in cleaner combustion . . . but only during high revs. Therefore, for normal stop-and-go "street" driving . . . and for those owners who are concerned about vehicle warranty . . . adhere to factory specs and emission system. But for weekend trips to the strips, try these "Staged-Tuning" tricks. Factory engineers have tested them to give you the ultimate output from your 302 BOSS. In fact, a "Plain Jane" 1968 Mustang with these mods around Dearborn earned the title "White Flash" because of the number of cars it put down. You can do the same. But remember this big clue. The "Staged-Tuning" tricks work TOGETHER . . . not independently of each other. They've been broken down into stages in keeping with the Muscle Parts concept. For maximum output, perform all of the modifications.

stage 1
induction
add 12 bhp and startling response

These modifications are relatively simple and inexpensive. Essentially, they involve a stronger and richer flow of gas and a horsepower gain by disconnecting the Thermactor pump. Recalibrating the carburetor adds a small amount of horsepower throughout the power range, but is most noticeable as added response at the bottom end. On the other hand, the Thermactor pump subtracts a negligible degree of Bhp under 5000 rpm, but pulls as much as 7 horsepower at 7000 rpm.

main metering jets

Production 780 cfm Holley's come with No. 68 primary jets and No. 82 secondary jets. As a starter, enrichen these about two numbers . . . No. 70 primary and No. 84 secondary respectively. However, as explained on pages 13 and 20-21 of original Muscle Parts book, final carburetor calibration may be affected by temperature, humidity and altitude. So for maximum performance a degree of trial and error is required here.

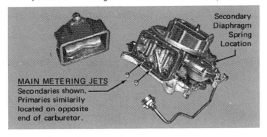

Secondary Diaphragm Spring Location

MAIN METERING JETS
Secondaries shown.
Primaries similarly located on opposite end of carburetor.

diaphragm spring

A stronger squirt of gas can be obtained by using a weaker diaphragm spring. They are serviced in a package of six different sizes under Holley part number 85BP-3185. Remove the stock "blue" spring, and install the service one color-coded "yellow".

heat riser

To provide satisfactory cold engine warm up, the heat riser passage conducts hot gases from one head to the other through the intake manifold. Warming the incoming air/fuel mixture is desireable for normal passenger car use, but for maximum performance COLD air is preferred because it contains more power-producing oxygen. To block the heat riser passage, use two stainless steel plates about 2" x 2" x 0.005" thick. Remove the intake manifold and install plates over by-pass cross-over passage in middle of both banks. Insert plates between the intake manifold gasket and cylinder head face. If they won't stay in place until manifold is tightened down, use something sticky such as sealer or adhesive.

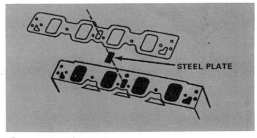

STEEL PLATE

thermactor

As previously noted, the Thermactor pump doesn't reduce horsepower until after about 5000 rpm. However, since this is where the 302 BOSS really starts to hum, the pump should be deactivated. This can be accomplished at the strip by simply removing the belt . . . and then reinstalling it for street use. Of course, if you use the 302 BOSS for the strip only, then remove the pump, brackets and plumbing. Plug the fitting at the heads as shown in the illustration.

electric fuel pump

A vacuum operated fuel pump at the front of the engine sucks gas from the tank into the carburetor. To make sure its reservoir and lines from the tank are full during peak revs, leave the stock pump in place and also install a 5-6 psi electric pump as near as possible to the tank. That way you're really covered against starvation when all the chips are up for grabs. If you build an all-out machine, install TWO electric pumps as illustrated.

tuning for 6000-7300 Rpm

ignition timing

The parts discussed in this stage won't in themselves add horsepower. What they do is allow your engine to rev up to the 7000 rpm range, which permits other components to add significant Bhp increase.

distributor limiter

The first step in going for more revs is to disconnect the limiter. If the engine is to be used only at the strip, then remove the complete limiter system. Otherwise, simply tape back the leads.

spark plugs and wiring

For street use, the stock 14mm AF-32's are okay. But at the strip try a colder plug such as an AF-12 or 22. Gap the plugs to 0.030''–0.032''. CAUTION: If you modify with "Competition Only" race pistons, don't use these extended reach (Power Tip) plugs. Steel core wiring is recommended for serious racing as explained on page 30.

dual point distributor

The 302 BOSS comes from the factory with a dual point distributor, which delivers a hotter spark in the 5000 rpm range than the conventional single point setup. However, it's a dual advance type. Meaning it advances spark timing with a centrifugal weight system . . . and a vacuum diaphragm system.

Vacuum advance is achieved with an arm extending from the diaphragm that moves a "pivot" plate to advance the breaker points with respect to the distributor cam. This system works well for normal passenger car use up to around 6000 rpm. But in the 6000-7000 rpm range for performance applications, the "pivot" plate tends to bounce . . . causing slightly erratic spark timing.

Centrifugal advance, on the other hand, is achieved with weights that are forced out from the distributor shaft by centrifugal force . . . and pull against calibrated spring tension to advance the distributor cam. This more positive system permits more accurate spark timing at high rpm.

Although the vacuum advance system is desirable for drivability, economy and to help control emissions on the street, it's a hindrance for all-out revving at the strip or track. There are three options to change over to strictly centrifugal advance with Autolite pieces at the strip.

option 1

The simplest and least expensive method is to install DUAL POINT DISTRIBUTOR KIT, Part No. D0AZ-12A132-B in your stock 302 BOSS distributor. It contains dual point breaker assembly, spacer plate, springs, specs and installation instructions. NOTE: You also need a "standard" 13 degree CAM ASSEMBLY, Part No. C5AZ-12210-A. Some 302 BOSS engines come from the factory with a 13 degree cam, but it will not work with this dual point kit because the cam is a different height than the "standard" cam.

option 2

The above dual point kit (D0AZ-12A132-B) can also be installed in a 289 or 302 (std.) distributor. Again, you need a "standard" 13 degree cam. However, many engines come from the factory with this cam. Check as illustrated on page 10 to identify. This might be the way to go if you want one distributor for competition use, and then re-install your stock dual advance distributor for street use.

option 3

Install 289 HIGH PERFORMANCE DUAL POINT DISTRIBUTOR, Part No. C50Z-12127-E. This costs more bucks, but presents absolutely zero hassle.

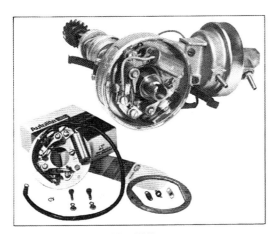

DUAL POINT DISTRIBUTOR CURVE

289 HP Distributor C50Z-12127-E and Kit D0AZ-12A132-B

Dist. rpm	250	500	1000	1500	2000	2500	3000	3500	4000
Dist. degrees	0°	3/4°	7°	8°	9°	10°	11°	12°	13°

installation tips

1. Dual point kit D0AZ-12A132-B contains several springs so it can also be used on 351 Windsor and 390/410/428 engines. ONLY USE THE SPRINGS SPECIFIED IN THE INSTRUCTIONS FOR EACH ENGINE. They are precisely calibrated to give the curve shown in the chart.

2. Do not modify the curve by installing weaker springs to achieve an earlier rise for more response. Instead, simply set the initial advance to 16 degrees at the crankshaft during idle. The dual point kit uses a distributor cam that permits a maximum advance of 13 degrees at 4000 distributor rpm. That's equivalent to 26 crank degrees at 8000 crank rpm. At 7000 crank rpm the advance is 24 crank degrees (12 distributor degrees). Adding the 16 degrees initial advance gives a total advance of 40 degrees at 7000 rpm . . . about the maximum recommended. If detonation occurs, retard the initial advance as necessary to prevent piston damage.

3. As explained in the instructions, set breaker point gap at 0.018" - 0.020" (25° dwell) for each point, and a combined total of 32-34 degrees dwell for both points.

4. When necessary to replace points, use 289 HP pieces, Part No. C3AZ-12171-A (2 sets). Check for 27-30 ounce tension. These are low-mass points to resist point bounce and the springs have a relatively high tension rate, so naturally they wear more rapidly than stock points.

distributor cam usage and identification

All Ford engines up through 1970 models use a 10-, 13- or 15-degree maximum advance distributor cam assembly. To identify each, look through the hole as illustrated. The plate of a 10- or 15- degree cam is stamped (10L - 15L) and a 13 degree cam (13L - 18L). All engines, except 302 BOSS, use a "standard" cam. A "standard" cam is located lower on the shaft than the 302 BOSS cam. Only a "standard" cam can be used with dual point kit D0AZ-12A132-B.

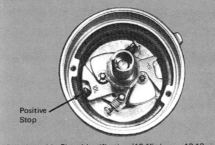

This plate is installed in the 10 degree position because the positive stop is in the 10 degree notch. To convert to a 15 degree plate, remove wick and retaining ring from top of shaft and rotate plate until positive stop is in 15 degree slot.

Positive Stop

Cam Assembly Plate Identification (10-15 shown, 13-18 similar)

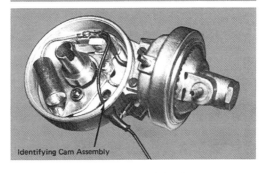

Identifying Cam Assembly

headers

Up to this point we've been talking about relatively inexpensive and simple modifications. Now we really make the 302 BOSS come alive with lightweight steel tube headers. They cost a few bucks, but are relatively cheap considering the way they improve performance. The factory "closed" exhaust system literally suffocates the big "let me breathe" ports. Headers reduce back pressure to the tune of about 15 horsepower @ 5000 rpm as conservatively measured on our dyno. A good tune job ought to pull more, especially at the top end. And headers improve response throughout the power range. Headers aren't available from Ford, but a number of companies manufacture them for the 302 BOSS. Dyno tests show that a primary tube measuring 34 inches long with a 2 inch I.D. into a 3-3 1/2 inch collector works best.

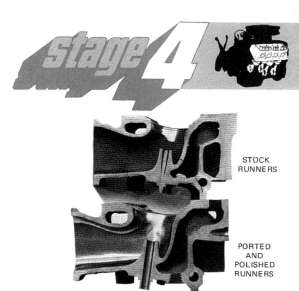

stage 4

ported 'n polished heads (optional)
add 15 horsepower

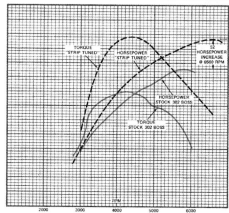

STOCK
RUNNERS

PORTED
AND
POLISHED
RUNNERS

This is an optional stage because ported and polished heads aren't legal in some drag classes. However, where legal they make a good modification as they add a conservative 15 Bhp at 5000 rpm. If this sounds like a small increase, remember that the 302 BOSS has very large ports in stock form. About all that is required is to clean up valve pocket areas, polish runners to remove any casting irregularities and do a typical progressive-cut performance valve job. These are detailed in the special "Boss 302 Engine Modification for Strip/Track" book described on page 5.

summing up

Here's some visual evidence of what you end up with. These are actual dyno curves, just in case you thought we are tossing numbers around off the top of our head. They indicate the MINIMUM torque and horsepower gained over a absolutely stock 302 BOSS engine when dyno-tuned and mechanically sound. You may add more or a little less depending on how close you stick to the critical dimensions in "clearancing" your engine.

stage 5

getting it all to the ground

Here are general chassis tips to get all that 302 BOSS power to the ground where it can do you some good. They've proven successful in stock BOSS 302 Mustang and Cougar Eliminator models. They also work for similar models in which a 302 BOSS engine is installed.

transmission

For faster "power" shifting, remove teeth from the second, third and fourth gear blocker rings.

rear axle gear

Since the 302 BOSS performs best when it's revving from 5000 to 7000 rpm, a high ratio gear is desirable. A 3.50 ratio comes standard, which is okay for expressway speeds, but around town a 4.30 works much better. For mostly strip use, a 4.57 or higher does the trick depending on tire diameter. The production "traction lok" is great for street use, but at the strip you need a "No-Spin" Detroit Locker differential, Part No. C3AZ-4880-B. It fits the stock 31-spline axle shafts and the 9-inch ring gear.

suspension

Install a good set of traction bars, spring clamps and pinion bumper to resist axle windup on acceleration and keep tires in maximum traction.

Lee Morse

Ken Miler, Crew Chief

Jacques Passino, Ford Executive

Parnelli Jones

Bud Moore

Bud's son Darrel

Fran Hernandez, Programme Manager

Winning the race and Championship at Riverside, CA in 1970

Chapter 12
Conclusion

With the desist racing instruction from upper management at Ford in November of 1970, there was little further action on the racing engine front from 1971 and none with regard to the small block Fairlane derived V8 engines until the 1980s. The activity of the previous nine years of 1962-1970 however had seen Ford ensure that the small block Ford engine had been highly successful in every class that it was entered in, especially those that had been factory backed. The first major factory backed racing application for this engine was the 1963 Indianapolis 500 engine which went remarkably well, with this version of the engine being developed to an incredibly high standard by Ford's engineers in a very short time.

The stock production 221ci and 260ci engines were not built with competition in mind, having been built as light in weight and as cheaply as possible to power intermediate road cars, and as a result of this, quite understandably, were not suitable with stock components for very much above this requirement. Ford for its part realised this and over time released special racing parts, but these were expensive; too expensive for most Ford car enthusiasts, especially when standard engines from other manufacturers were capable of about 500-1000rpm more without any parts substitution that involved an engine strip-down. When Ford built racing parts for these engines they were as good as – if not better than – the competition. It must also be said that its stock engines were without a doubt lighter and more compact than Ford's contemporaries, equalling or bettering all on the basis of reliability and economy due to outstanding design.

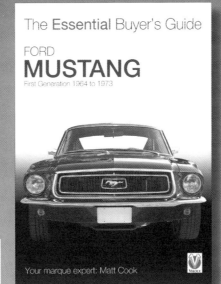

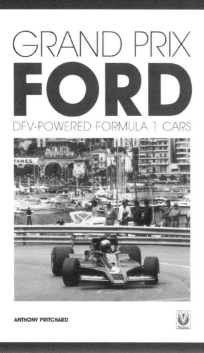

Also from Veloce Publishing ...

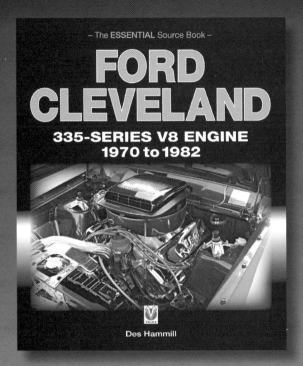

Ford Cleveland
335-Series V8 engine 1970 to 1982
Des Hammill

Years of meticulous research have resulted in this unique history, technical appraisal (including tuning and motorsports) and data book of the Ford V8 Cleveland 335 engines produced in the USA, Canada and Australia, including input from the engineers involved in the design, development and subsequent manufacture of this highly prized engine from its inception in 1968 until production ceased in 1982.

ISBN: 978-1-845843-49-6
• Paperback • 25x20.7cm • £14.99* UK/$29.95* USA
• 96 pages • 46 colour and b&w pictures

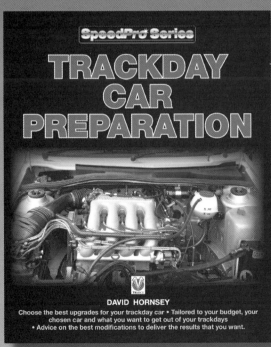

Trackday car preparation
David Hornsey

The perfect place to start your trackday experience. From helping you choose the best car and upgrades, to advice on insurance, trackday companies, trackdays abroad, and circuit driving techniques, this book is tailored to your needs and your budget – whether you're after fun, thrills, speed or all three!

ISBN: 978-1-845844-83-7
• Paperback • 25x20.7cm • £14.99* UK/$24.95* USA
• 96 pages • 90 colour pictures

*prices subject to change, p&p extra
For more details visit www.veloce.co.uk or email info@veloce.co.uk

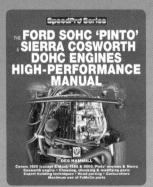

Index